This book is a gift to:

....

From:

....

Date:

....

THE ILLUSTRATED

Devotional

FOR

GIRLS

366 DAYS OF CREATIVE COLORING
& FAITH-FILLED DEVOTIONS

christian
art kids

Never Alone

Today is the first day of a new year. Sure, it is awesome … but sometimes new beginnings can be a little scary. Maybe you've moved to a new town and have to start over in a new school. Maybe your best friend moved away.

Is it hard to find God in the middle of all this? Today's Scripture promises that you will never be alone. God will be by your side and will guide you and help you to get through the scary times. You can rest assured that you will never need to face anything on your own.

Father,

Thank You for reminding me again and again that I can depend on You. You promise to NEVER leave me alone. Don't ever let me forget that.

Amen

Isaiah 43:2

Hamster-Wheel Living

Do you feel like a hamster running on an exercise wheel? You get up in the morning, go to school, sit through classes, come home, do homework, have dinner, go to bed and get up in the morning to start all over again.

This hamster-wheel living gets pretty old. You might be tempted to look for some excitement in places where you shouldn't. Jesus offers a better way 'cause He gives you the chance to let Him take care of your problems.

Trust Him to take care of life and you just enjoy it.

Dear Lord,

Knowing I can give my problems to You feels like taking a deep breath of cool, fresh air. Help me to leave them with You ... and just trust You to take care of them.   Amen

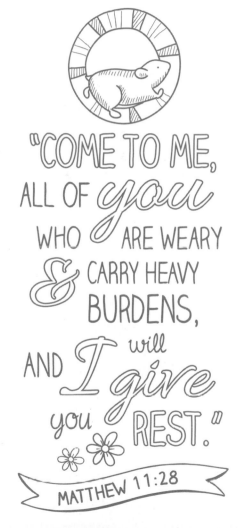

"COME TO ME, ALL OF *you* WHO ARE WEARY & CARRY HEAVY BURDENS, AND *I will give you* REST."

MATTHEW 11:28

Brokenhearted

THE
BROKENHEARTED
& binds
UP THEIR
WOUNDS.
PSALM 147:3

People you thought were your friends, in fact, who used to be your friends, suddenly start ganging up on you. They won't talk to you. You see them huddling together and giggling. You haven't done anything. Nothing is different, but all of a sudden you're out and they're in. It hurts, doesn't it?

How do you handle this? You might feel like pond scum; you might start ugly rumors about your old friends. Better idea: Instead of getting down on yourself or them, talk to God about what's going on. He cares about your feelings and your loneliness.

He will heal your broken heart. He will surround you with His love. Tell Him how you're feeling. He cares.

Dear Father,

Thank You for caring. It really hurts when my friends are mean to me. Please help me find good friends.

Amen

Putting on God's Armor

It may be freaky to think about, but sometimes the lousy things of life are caused by the devil! He wants to make sure that your friendship with God doesn't grow. He wants to make sure that you don't tell other people that God loves them. So he keeps you busy mucking through the junk of life. He knows if he keeps you discouraged or busy, you won't have time for the good stuff.

So how do you fight the devil? By putting on God's armor. Ephesians 6 tells us how to wear the belt of truth, breastplate of righteousness, shield of faith, helmet of salvation – everything you need to make the devil turn around and run like a scared cat.

Dear God,

It's cool to know that the armor is there waiting for me. I want to use it. Help me to put it on.

Amen

Put on the FULL ARMOR of GOD, so that you can take your stand against the devil's schemes.

EPHESIANS 6:11

Hard Times

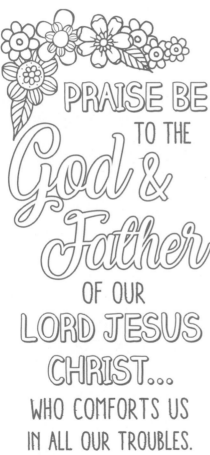

PRAISE BE TO THE God & Father OF OUR LORD JESUS CHRIST... WHO COMFORTS US IN ALL OUR TROUBLES.

2 CORINTHIANS 1:3-4

Did you expect that when you became a Christian, God would stop your problems? Things don't work that way. Sometimes bad things happen and God doesn't stop them. But He never leaves you alone to go through hard times.

Maybe you think that if God stopped bad things from happening, then people would see how powerful He is. Guess what? Sometimes people see God's power by watching you!

They see how real faith works as you trust Him and allow Him to comfort and teach you through the stinky times of life.

Dear God,

I'm going to need Your help in a major way. If others are going to see Your power in me when life stinks ... help me to trust You more every day.

Amen

Turn to God

Where do you go for help when you're feeling crummy? Do you turn to your friends? To sports? To magazines? If any of those things are your answer to problems, you're probably still looking for comfort. God is the most powerful, loving and caring being in your whole life.

Turn to Him for help and comfort and you will find someone who will hold on to you no matter how hard life gets. You'll find in Him someone who can actually DO something about the not-so-nice stuff and someone who will love you all the way through it.

God is a rock ... a fortress. Pretty strong, huh?

Dear God,

Sometimes I've looked in the wrong places for help and strength. Forgive me. Help me to find my strength in You. *Amen*

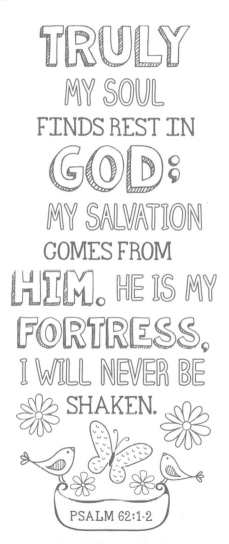

TRULY MY SOUL FINDS REST IN GOD; MY SALVATION COMES FROM HIM. HE IS MY FORTRESS, I WILL NEVER BE SHAKEN.

PSALM 62:1-2

No Surprises

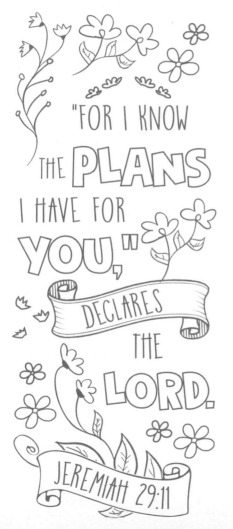

"FOR I KNOW THE PLANS I HAVE FOR YOU," DECLARES THE LORD.

JEREMIAH 29:11

Nothing that happens to you is a surprise to God ... nothing. He has plans for you that were laid out before you ever even opened your eyes for the first time on this earth.

His plans are to bring good into your life. A promise of hope that will lead all the way to heaven and a future with Him forever.

Your part in this plan is simply to listen to Him and follow Him. Read His Word, pray, be still and listen for His voice in your heart.

More than anything, trust Him ... even through the hard times ... even when you can't see a light at the end of the tunnel, trust God's heart.

Dear Father,

I'm so glad You have a plan for my life. I'm glad You're in control.

Amen

Knowing Him

You can trust God. That's the bottom line. No matter what life throws you; no matter how many bad choices you make; no matter how lousy your attitude is ... you can trust God.

Do those words really mean anything to you? A skydiver wouldn't jump out of a plane without testing his parachute. A racecar driver wouldn't drive 200 miles per hour without testing his car. They know their equipment.

If you're going to give your life to God shouldn't you know Him? Read His Word to see how He has taken care of His people in the past. Be quiet before Him, let Him speak to your heart. The better you know Him, the more you will trust Him.

Dear Father,

I want to know You better and better. Help me learn to love Your Word and to love spending quiet time with You. *Amen*

The LORD is GOOD, a STRONGHOLD IN THE DAY of trouble.

nahum 1:7

Good from Bad

FOR THOSE WHO Love GOD all things work TOGETHER FOR GOOD.

ROMANS 8:28

Aaaaarrrggghhh! Does this verse make you want to scream, "How can you say that God can work good from my junk?" Go ahead and yell ... you'll feel better.

Now, listen to this ... God may not stop your parents' divorce. He may not give you great grades, lots of friends, amazing sports ability, or a job for your dad. He might, but He also just might not. However, what He will definitely do, if you will let Him, is work in your heart to make your faith stronger. He will show you that you can depend on Him. As you see Him doing these things, you will know more than ever that He loves you.

Cool, huh?

Dear God,

Help me to see You in my life. Help me to recognize Your love and care even when things aren't going great. Thanks for always being there.

Amen

Three-in-One

*I*s your life kind of a mess? Whose fault do you think that is? Come on, be honest, have you been blaming everyone around you for your problems and not accepting any of the responsibility yourself? Who made the choices that got you where you are? Who decided to act like a jerk to others, cheat on tests, yell at Mom and Dad ... or whatever it is that makes your life stink? You did, right?

Well, maybe you finally feel that it's time to behave and make wise choices, but you just don't know how. Proverbs 2:6 has the answer – ask God. He will give you wisdom, knowledge and understanding – three for the price of one! Go ahead and ask – He wants to give it to you!

Dear God,

Forgive me for the bad choices I've made. Help me to make better ones. Guide my thoughts.

Amen

THE LORD GIVES WISDOM; FROM HIS MOUTH COME KNOWLEDGE & UNDERSTANDING.
PROVERBS 2:6

Who Ya Gonna Call?

THE
LORD
IS MY
STRENGTH & MY
SHIELD;
MY
HEART
TRUSTS
IN HIM.
PSALM 28:7

*I*t's time for some soul-searching. Does this kind of thing ever happen in your family: Mom asks you to do something and you respond with, "Okay, in a minute." However, that minute never comes. Mom keeps asking and you keep putting her off. You are turning a deaf ear to her.

Thank goodness God never does that to you. When you're having problems or when you feel stuck in the stinkiness of life, you can call on God for help. You can call over and over and over. In fact, that's what He wants you to do. He will help you – He promised.

Dear God,

This is so awesome. I can ask You for help every single day ... in fact, You want me to. Thank You so much.

Amen

Life Focus

*W*hat is the absolute most important thing in your life right now? Come on, be honest. Do you dream about being super popular; do you want to be the best at every school subject; or do you want to be a better athlete or musician? Where do you put your energy and attention?

Whatever occupies your attention, your thoughts – that's what you're serving and whatever you are serving will determine how your life is going.

Here's a thought – choose God. Yeah, choose to put your energy and time into getting to know Him better. Choose to serve Him by learning His Word and by letting Him guide your life. You'll find that life will go a lot better when God is at the center of it.

Dear Father,

Help me to put my energy into knowing You better. I want You to be the most important thing in my life. *Amen*

BUT AS FOR ME & MY HOUSE, WE WILL SERVE THE LORD.

Joshua 24:15

Speech Lessons

THE MOUTHS OF FOOLS ARE THEIR UNDOING.

PROVERBS 18:7

*H*ey, did ya hear about Rachel and Jason? Well, I heard ... " GOSSIP! It's so tempting, but it can get you in such trouble. It can wreck friendships, ruin reputations – for both those gossiped about *and* those who do the gossiping.

Things said about others and things said in anger will come back to haunt you. Friendships will be wrecked. After all, who wants to be friends with someone who is mean. People won't trust you with their secrets or respect what you think or say.

The best thing to do is to watch what you say – you know the famous old saying from mothers around the world ... "If you haven't got something good to say, don't say anything at all!" Mothers are so wise.

Dear God,

I really need help learning this lesson. Please help me by guarding my mouth for me. Thanks.

Amen

No Matter What

Sometimes life is hard. The truth is that it can sometimes get so hard that it feels like God has turned His back on you; like He doesn't know what you're going through.

No matter how hard life gets; how alone you feel; how discouraged you are, remember this: GOD LOVES YOU! Nothing can change that.

He's holding on to you, even if it doesn't "feel" like it sometimes. Trust His Word. It promises that His love is forever!

Dear God,

Thank You, thank You, thank You for loving me ... forever and always!   *Amen*

I AM CONVINCED THAT NEITHER DEATH NOR LIFE, NOR ANYTHING ELSE IN ALL CREATION, WILL BE ABLE TO SEPARATE US FROM THE LOVE OF GOD.

ROMANS 8:38-39

Think Good Thoughts

Whatever is TRUE,
Whatever is HONORABLE,
Whatever is JUST,
Whatever is LOVELY,
Whatever is COMMENDABLE ...
THINK about these things.

Philippians 4:8

Garbage in ... garbage out. The stuff you let wander through your thoughts on a regular basis soon settles in your heart, then begins to form who you are and what shape your life takes.

Don't play dumb – you know the difference between right and wrong. If you don't, spend some time reading God's Word and you'll begin to understand what is true, noble, right, pure, lovely and admirable.

If you'd be embarrassed for your parents to know what you're thinking ... or even worse, if Jesus knew, then it's wrong. Putting better things in your mind will bring better things out.

Dear Father,

I'm sorry for the things I let run around in my mind sometimes. Please help me to focus my thoughts on good things. Amen

Honesty

So, you've got problems ... well, so does everyone else. Does that surprise you? Did you think you were the only one? Maybe that's because some people pretend that everything in life is great.

You can pretend for people and even fool them for a long time ... but you can't fool God for a minute. He knows what's going on in your heart. He knows if you're happy, sad, mad, depressed or hopeless.

Don't bother pretending. Just tell God the truth – even if you've caused the messes yourself. That's what humbling yourself means – admitting your mistakes. He will lift you out of the messes and set you on the right path.

Dear God,

I'm glad You know my mistakes. I'm glad I don't have to try to hide things from You. Please help me fix the things I've messed up and give me a fresh start.

Amen

HUMBLE yourselves before the LORD and He will EXALT YOU.

JAMES 4:10

No Worries

"I WILL BE WITH YOU. I will not leave you or forsake YOU."

JOSHUA 1:5

More than likely you know some people who just like to make others miserable. They make fun of your clothes, your grades, your body, your family, even your walk with God.

Some kids even try to get you to do things you know you shouldn't. Yeah, well as you get older, those kinds of people keep coming at you. Does that make the future look scary?

Hey, no worries – you aren't alone. God promises to be with you every step in life – today, tomorrow and forever. He *promised* that He will never leave you on your own. So, turn away from the creeps who want to knock you down and turn to God for help and strength.

Dear God,

I'm so glad to know that You will never leave me. I know You will help me face whatever life brings. Thank You.

Amen

It Never Runs Out

Do you love home-made cookies? Do you like to bake? Did you ever start making cookies ... get all the ingredients out, measure the sugar, mix in the butter ... and then find out you don't have enough flour to finish the recipe? It's frustrating to run out of something and not be able to finish what you've started.

It's nice to know that will never happen with God. You can go to Him, ask for His help and know that His wisdom and knowledge will never run out. Every minute of every hour of every day His well will *never* go dry.

So, ask God's help, His knowledge about the future, His wisdom for your choices. Go often and listen closely.

Dear God,

I know You always finish what You start. That includes Your plan for my life. Help me to pay attention to everything You say. *Amen*

Oh, the depth of the riches of the wisdom and knowledge of God.

Romans 11:33

Floating Feathers

"Before I *formed* you in the *womb* I knew *you*."

Jeremiah 1:5

A feather floating through the air soars up and down, right and left. It's hard to guess where it will land. Do you ever feel that your life is on a feather's journey? Some days you make good choices and some days you mess up. You like piano and soccer. You excel at math, but stink at English. How is it all going to fit together?

You aren't in this floating feather journey alone, you know. God has known you since before you first uttered a sound. He has a plan for your life. Your responsibility is to stay close to Him – talk to Him every day, listen for Him to speak to you, read His Word, seek His guidance.

Here's a tip: Turn off your phone, shut down the computer. Close your door and spend alone time with God.

Dear Lord,

Help me to learn how to be quiet and listen to You. Speak to me through Your Word. *Amen*

Ultimate Future

*L*et's be honest ... sometimes life stinks. Parents who fight a lot; money problems; problems with friends. Maybe you're failing at school ... whatever it is; it's hard. Is it hard to think about the future because you're scared things may not get better?

There is an ultimate stopping point – one place in the future where there will only be good.

Christ promised that He would come back for His children and take them to heaven someday. If He cares enough to do that for you, it's reasonable to believe that He loves you enough to care for you day in and day out here, too.

Dear God,

Knowing You love me makes the future a lot less scary. Thank You for loving me. *Amen*

"IF I GO AND PREPARE A place FOR you, I WILL COME AGAIN AND WILL TAKE YOU TO Myself."

JOHN 14:3

Joy in Darkness

Though you have not SEEN HIM, YOU love HIM.

1 Peter 1:8

It's late. Your room is dark ... so is your soul. You feel alone and hopeless. It seems like no one knows what you're going through, or if they know, they just don't care. Suddenly, far away in the darkness, you see a little pinprick of light.

Slowly it moves closer and closer. What is it? Hope. Hope that comes because, even though you haven't seen God face to face, you love Him and you *know* that He loves you. He never leaves you alone. He always cares about what you're feeling.

Dear God,

Help me to remember that I'm never alone – You are always with me. Thanks for that. It makes me feel better to know You are there. *Amen*

Choosing the Better Way

So, you love those who love you ... you're friendly to your friends ... you do nice things for those who do nice things for you. Big deal. Anyone can do that.

It's when life gets tough, when someone tells lies about you, cheats you, steals from you, or is just generally a jerk that you have a choice to make.

You can decide to be just as stinky as they are and let your behavior sink to their level, or you can choose to behave like God's child and love your enemy, even pray for them.

It's a choice you have to make every day.

Dear God,

Please help me to treat others the way You want me to. Help me to show love, even to those who are mean to me. *Amen*

"LOVE your enemies & PRAY for those who persecute you, that you may be children of your Father in heaven."

matthew 5:44-45

A Fresh Heart

The **heart** is deceitful *above* all things and beyond cure. Who can understand it?

♥ Jeremiah 17:9 ♥

Have you ever opened a new bag of apples and found one right in the middle that's totally rotten? Did you notice how all the apples around that one are beginning to rot, too? Yeah, rottenness spreads. The same is true of what's in your heart. Have you been complaining that your life is rotten – things are just not going well?

Stop and look at your own heart. If there is hatred, selfishness, lies, deceit or other rottenness living there, that will come out in your life. Maybe some of your problems could possibly be your own fault. So maybe it would be a good idea to stop complaining about others or about your situation, and clean up your heart – admit sinfulness, confess it and repent. Start fresh.

Dear God,

It's hard to admit the wrong things I've done. But, I want to ... and to ask forgiveness. Please help me start fresh today.

Amen

Growing Stronger

No one likes to hurt or have problems. We'll do just about anything to stop pain. For physical pain, you take medicine. For emotional pain, you either blame someone or get help. You just want it to stop. Look at nature though ... the pressure of tons of weight turns ordinary minerals into diamonds; gold has to be purified in a hot, hot fire; young trees that are blown around by stormy winds are actually strengthened.

God says that the same is true of us. Problems can make us stronger because every time our faith in God is tested and we see Him come through, we trust Him more. So, instead of trying to get away from problems, see what you can learn from them.

Dear God,

This is kind of a hard thing to learn. But help me to learn from hard times. Help me trust You more. Help my faith to grow stronger. *Amen*

CONSIDER IT PURE JOY

WHENEVER YOU FACE TRIALS OF MANY KINDS, BECAUSE YOU KNOW THAT

THE TESTING OF YOUR FAITH PRODUCES PERSEVERANCE. JAMES 1:2–3

The Heart of Jesus

When the **Lord saw her, His heart** went out to her and He said, "Don't cry."

Luke 7:13

If you ever wonder if God cares about what you're going through, read through the Gospels and see how Jesus felt about the people who were suffering.

This verse from Luke is from the time when Jesus met a widow whose only son had just died. This shows you the heart of Jesus – His heart went out to her. He felt bad for her and wanted to make her situation better.

The Gospels are filled with stories of Jesus helping people who were in pain. His character hasn't changed in 2,000 years. He still cares, His heart still goes out to you when you're hurting.

Don't ever think that Jesus doesn't care. He does. He may not always take your problems away, but He will walk through them with you.

Dear Father,

Thank You for caring about me when I'm hurting. Thank You for always being with me. *Amen*

Open Ears

How do you feel about a friend who is always complaining? Someone who has one problem after another?

Even if they are legitimate problems, do you get tired of hearing about them? Do you kind of stay away from that person? Yeah, probably. Hearing about other people's problems all the time gets old.

But isn't it great to know that God doesn't do that? He never gets sick of hearing about your problems or your pleas for help. He cares. You can go to God over and over and over. He cares.

He will listen and He will help you through your problems.

Dear God,

I know I complain a lot. I know I'm always asking You to help with things. Thank You that You never stop caring or listening ... or helping.

Amen

FOR HE HAS NOT DESPISED OR SCORNED THE SUFFERING OF THE AFFLICTED ONE...

BUT HAS LISTENED TO HIS CRY FOR HELP.

PSALM 22:24

Cleaned-Up Hearts

"I WILL cleanse YOU from all your impurities and from all your idols."

Ezekiel 36:25

As you get to know God better by reading His Word, you will learn that sometimes your life is stinky because of choices you make. The heart that doesn't know and serve God is wicked. It makes selfish and sometimes rotten choices. The hope that God offers is that you do not have to stay that way.

When you ask Jesus into your heart, He will cleanse it. He promises to take away the urge to do wrong. He'll even help you change the idols in your life — things that pull your heart away from God. Your responsibility in this is to stay close to Him by reading His Word, talking to Him and listening to Him.

Dear God,

There is always something that is trying to pull me away from You. I need Your help to stick close to You. I can't do it by myself. Amen

Stop the Madness!

Okay, so your friends are acting like jerks. All of a sudden, they want nothing to do with you. They lie to you about when and where they're hanging out. They spread rumors about you – out and out lies! How are you going to respond?

You could do just exactly what they are doing: Keep the cycle going by gathering a new group of friends around you and telling lies about your old friends, treating them like jerks ... OR ... you could do what God suggests.

Stop the cycle and make the effort to make things better by loving your old friends. Just loving them. That's what God says will work. He should know, He wrote the book on love!

Dear God,

I'm going to need Your help big time on this one. Help me to love my enemies. I can't do it without Your help. *Amen*

"Love your neighbor as yourself. I am the LORD."

Leviticus 19:18

Never Beaten

> WE ARE HARD PRESSED ON EVERY SIDE, BUT NOT CRUSHED;
>
> PERPLEXED, BUT NOT IN DESPAIR;
>
> PERSECUTED, BUT NOT ABANDONED.
>
> 2 CORINTHIANS 4:8-9

God never promised to take away all your problems. Just because you become a Christian doesn't mean that you can just settle down with a diet cola and expect God to make everything wonderful.

What you can count on is that God knows that sometimes you have problems, He knows that other kids pick on you, He knows there are problems at home or school. He knows.

Not only does He know, He cares. You can count on Him to stick with you through all the junk of life. He'll be your strength, He'll show you how to act and react to others. You will not be abandoned or destroyed by anything life brings.

Dear Father,

Well, to tell the truth, I'd rather have You take away all my problems. But, if that isn't going to happen, I'm glad that You are here to help me through them. Thanks. *Amen*

Hang in There

You go to church; say a "thanks" prayer before lunch; you choose to stay away from destructive behavior; you choose not to use God's name as a swear word; you choose not to rip up others' reputations. You make all these choices because you're a Christian, a child of God who wants to obey Him and live the way He commands.

Be warned – these choices may tick off other people because you don't make the same kinds of choices they do. They may try to make your life completely miserable just because you are a Christian.

Don't worry – God knows what is going on. He promises to bless you because you've made the right choices. Hang in there.

Dear God,

I want to make the right choices. I want people to know that I'm Your child. Help me be strong when the going gets tough. *Amen*

"BLESSED are you when people insult you, persecute you and falsely say all kinds of evil against YOU because of ME."

Matthew 5:11

Take Responsibility

A PERSON'S OWN FOLLY LEADS TO THEIR RUIN, YET THEIR HEART RAGES AGAINST THE LORD.

PROVERBS 19:3

Do you blame someone else for your problems? The crummier life gets, do you try harder to blame someone else? Your problems are never your fault, right? They didn't happen because of choices you've made. Yeah, right. Sometimes life stinks because you've made bad choices – about how to treat other people, where to spend your time and energy, where to put your interests – and you pay the price for those choices.

Don't try to blame God because your life stinks. First, accept responsibility for your choices. Once you confess your sins and repent He will be right there to help you pick up the pieces and start fresh.

Dear God,

I've made some really dumb choices and they are the reasons for some of the problems in my life. I'm sorry. Help me make better choices.

Amen

February

Learning Curve

The Beginning

In the beginning, GOD created the HEAVENS and the EARTH.

Genesis 1:1

Everything began with God. Before He started creating the world, there wasn't any earth, trees, sky, people, animals – nothing.

Look around you at the world He made ... what a powerful God. Not just powerful either, He pays attention to every detail.

He knows the biggest things in the world and the smallest. He made you. He loves you. He has a plan for your life. He's worth getting to know. The Bible is His story and by reading it you will learn how He has taken care of His people and how He will take care of you and love you more than you can even imagine.

Dear God,

When I stop and think about Your power and Your creativity, I'm blown away that You care about me. It's amazing ... and I'm so thankful that You do.

Amen

In God's Image

Okay, you have bad days, weeks, months. You may even sometimes feel like you are just one big mess with no reason for being here and with no purpose on earth.

Well, these ten words spoken by God prove that isn't true. You are made in God's image. Think about that for a minute. He is wisdom, love, power, creativity ... anything you can think of is possible in you because all of it was made *by* God and *is* God.

All of that was put into Adam and Eve – your ancestors. God made you and He gave you unique abilities and talents – just like Him! Cool, huh?

Dear God,

Sometimes I feel so useless and dumb. When I start feeling that way, remind me that I'm made in Your image and that means I'm worth something! You didn't make any garbage!

Amen

Then God said, "Let us make MANKIND in our IMAGE, in our LIKENESS."

Genesis 1:26

You Can't Fool God

THE **LORD GOD** BANISHED HIM FROM THE **GARDEN** OF **EDEN** TO WORK THE GROUND FROM WHICH HE HAD BEEN **TAKEN.**

GENESIS 3:23

*H*ave you ever tried to get away with something? Come on, be straight – your mom or dad tells you, "Do this" or "Don't do that" but you do exactly what you're not supposed to do. Then you try to lie your way out of it or blame someone else ... anything to avoid punishment.

Adam and Eve tried that after breaking the one rule God gave them. It didn't work, though. God knew exactly what they had done and He punished them for it.

God doesn't take disobedience. He punishes it. He sent Adam and Eve out of the Garden of Eden. Don't ever think you can fool God. You can't.

Dear God,

I know there isn't any chance at all of fooling You. Well, the truth is that I don't want to fool You. Please help me be honest with You all the time.

Amen

Count on It

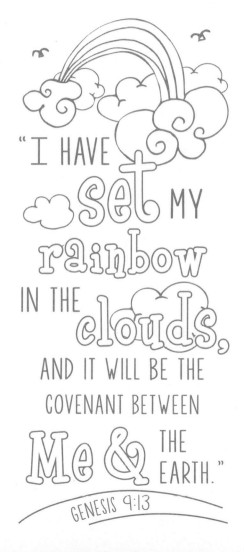

"I HAVE SET MY rainbow IN THE clouds, AND IT WILL BE THE COVENANT BETWEEN Me & THE EARTH."

GENESIS 9:13

*P*romises. They are great if they are kept. But if you have ever been the victim of a broken promise, you know how much it hurts and how hard it is to trust the promise-maker the next time.

If you've ever been the promise-breaker you have probably learned that your friends don't trust you so readily the next time.

God makes promises. This one from Genesis is the one He made with mankind through Noah. The rainbow is the sign of this promise. One thing you can count on with God – He keeps His promises ... always. Count on it.

Dear God,

Sometimes I start to feel about You the way I feel about people. Then I wonder if I can trust You – if You will always keep Your word. Thanks for this reminder that You mean what You say ... I can count on it.   *Amen*

Never Alone

God said, "I will be with you."

Exodus 3:12

Those are five pretty powerful words, aren't they? God said them to Moses, right after He gave Moses a job to do. Moses was scared that he couldn't handle the job, but God reminded him that he wasn't alone.

God's Word is filled with that same promise to you ... God will be with you. Whatever life brings, whatever job God gives you to do, you don't have to handle it alone.

That's comforting when you feel you aren't up to the job, or that you don't have the brains or strength or creativity to do the job before you.

God didn't just toss you into this world and say, "You're on your own!" Nope, He's with you every step of the way, giving guidance, strength ... whatever you need. He promised!

Dear God,

Thanks. I'm glad that You are always with me. I don't know what I'd do without You. Amen

Miracle Worker

More tension than any movie or TV show – God frees the Israelites from slavery and Egypt, and Moses leads them into the wilderness. Then the Egyptian king decides he wants them back and sends his whole army after them.

So, the Israelites are stuck with the Red Sea behind them and the Egyptian army in front of them ... hopeless, right?

Not when God is on your side. He parted the waters and they walked right through. God can do whatever He needs to do to protect you, help you, guide you.

Pay attention to your life every day and you just might see God commanding the unusual on your behalf!

Dear God,

Wow! I'm going to keep my eyes open every day to see what You might do to take care of me!

Amen

THE ISRAELITES WENT THROUGH THE SEA ON DRY GROUND WITH A WALL OF WATER ON THEIR RIGHT AND ON THEIR LEFT.
EXODUS 14:22

Big and Little

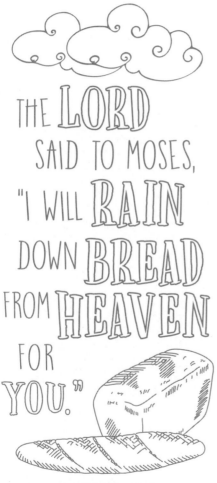

THE **LORD** SAID TO MOSES, "I WILL **RAIN** DOWN **BREAD** FROM **HEAVEN** FOR **YOU.**

EXODUS 16:4

Do you sometimes wonder if God really cares about the little things that worry you? Does He only care about the big spiritual things or do things like whether or not you have food, friends, what sports you play, how you treat others, or topics for papers you must write mean anything to Him? He cares about everything.

Look what He did for the Israelites. They were wandering around in the wilderness and they ran out of food. They got hungrier and hungrier so He rained down bread, called manna, from heaven for them.

God took care of their immediate need and He will do the same for you. Tell Him what you need.

Dear God,

It's amazing that You care about the things that I worry about – even the little things. Thank You for caring and for helping. *Amen*

Out of the Mouth ...

Maybe you're wondering what those words have to do with you. After all, God didn't bring you out of Egypt or free you from slavery.

Well, these are the words God spoke as He began writing the Ten Commandments on tablets of stone. Yeah, you're probably paying more attention now, aren't you?

The Ten Commandments are God's guidelines for how we should treat one another and God. If everyone would just live by these simple guidelines the world would be a much happier place. Give it a try. Read Exodus 20 and see how you match up with obeying the Ten Commandments.

Dear God,

Sometimes I think I'm doing pretty good, but when I honestly look at the Ten Commandments and how I obey them ... I kind of stink. Help me to live by them. I know I'd be happier and so would everyone around me. *Amen*

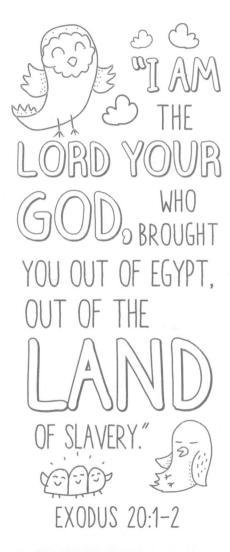

"I AM THE LORD YOUR GOD, WHO BROUGHT YOU OUT OF EGYPT, OUT OF THE LAND OF SLAVERY."

EXODUS 20:1–2

Stay Strong

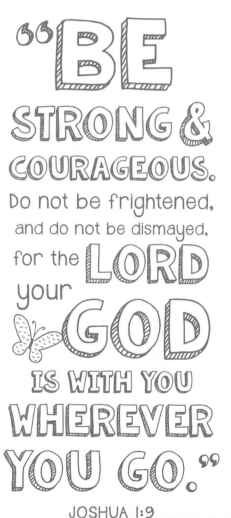

"BE STRONG & COURAGEOUS. Do not be frightened, and do not be dismayed, for the LORD your GOD IS WITH YOU WHEREVER YOU GO."

JOSHUA 1:9

The Israelites had followed Moses for a long time through some tough things. But, now he was dead and Joshua was in charge. Why should the people listen to him? Why should they do anything he said? He could have been shaking in his boots – except for these few words from God.

About three times in the first chapter of Joshua God told the new leader to be strong and courageous. He had nothing to be afraid of – God was with him.

The same thing holds true for you – if other kids give you a hard time, if unbelieving family members push you around – don't be afraid. No matter what you face, you're not alone. God is with you wherever you go!

Dear God,

Keep reminding me that I'm not alone. Sometimes life is hard and I don't think I can make it by myself. It's good to know that I don't have to.

Amen

Shower Time

*I*magine taking a nice hot shower using your favorite sweet-smelling shower gel. After the shower you dry yourself with a nasty towel and put on dirty stinky clothes. That just made the shower a waste of time, didn't it? That kind of describes what Joshua was telling his people in this verse.

Clean yourselves up, confess your sin, turn away from it, humble yourselves before God ... and stay clean. He said they would then see God do amazing things for them.

Do you want God to do amazing things in your life? Well, your heart and life clean up must come first ... get busy ... then you will see God do amazing things!

Dear God,

I want to see You do amazing things in my life. Help me. Show me how to clean up my life and help me learn to humble myself before You.

Amen

Consecrate yourselves, for tomorrow the LORD will do amazing things among you.

Joshua 3:5

Second Chances

"O Lord GOD, please (remember) me & please strengthen me."

Judges 16:28

Do you know who spoke these words? Samson – the strongest man who ever walked the earth. God blessed Samson with incredible strength; as long as he lived by the rules God gave him.

Of course, Samson broke the rules and was captured by his enemies. But Samson learned a lesson. He recognized that his strength and power didn't come from his muscles or his good looks – it came from God. So, he asked for another chance and God gave it to him. He helped Samson, blind and in chains, defeat his powerful enemies.

God loves you and wants you to succeed in life. Keep asking for His help and live the way He tells you to live. Keep asking.

Dear God,

I mess up so often. I'm sorry. I'm so sorry. Please forgive me and give me another chance.

Amen

God Hears You

Sometimes it feels like your prayers don't get past the ceiling, right? Not so, my friend. He hears.

God spoke these words just before He gave the Israelites the king they had been begging for. He heard their prayers and responded. God always hears. Sometimes He answers right away with a resounding "yes." Sometimes He takes His time and gives you a chance to discover whether that prayer is really something you want. Sometimes He protects you from your own foolishness and simply says, "No."

Whatever His answer, be sure of this – your prayers do not fall on deaf ears or an uncaring heart.

Dear God,

Thank You for hearing my prayers. Thank You for caring about the things that are on my mind and heart.

Amen

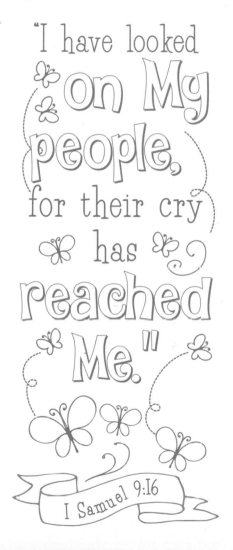

"I have looked on My people, for their cry has reached Me."

I Samuel 9:16

David and Goliath

YOU COME AGAINST ME WITH **SWORD** & **SPEAR** AND **JAVELIN,** **BUT** I COME AGAINST YOU IN THE **NAME** OF THE LORD **ALMIGHTY,** THE **GOD** OF THE ARMIES OF ISRAEL, WHOM YOU HAVE DEFIED.

1 SAMUEL 17:45

David and Goliath. The classic story of big battling little and little coming out on top. The story of David and Goliath from the world's point of view finds no reason David should win.

Goliath was bigger, stronger, had more experience. He had armor and a shield and spear. David had ... a sling and stones. But David knew that he had God on his side and no sword, spear or javelin had a chance against the Almighty God.

So, what does this mean for you? Plain talk – what tough things are you facing? From family problems to your own self-esteem ... come to the battle in the name of the Lord Almighty. Nothing can stand against that!

Dear God,

Thanks for being on my side. I want to always live and fight in Your name. Help me stay close to You.

Amen

Wise Choices

If you could have anything in the world, what would you want? Think a minute before you answer. Would you ask for fame? Wealth? Would you want that creep in homeroom to be covered with pimples?

God told King Solomon to ask for anything he wanted. Solomon wanted to be a good leader for his people so he asked God to make him wise.

God was pleased with his choice so He made Solomon wise ... and rich beyond his wildest dreams. God honors wise choices. If you're asking God to bless your decisions and the choices you make, make sure that you think of others before yourself.

Dear God,

I don't mean to always think about myself first. Help me to think about others and to do things that will help them. *Amen*

"BEHOLD, I GIVE YOU A WISE AND DISCERNING MIND."

1 KINGS 3:12

Never Too Young

WHO knows whether you have not come to **the kingdom** FOR SUCH A **TIME** as this?

Esther 4:14

Hey – I'm just a kid. I want to have fun. I'll think about important stuff when I'm older. Sound familiar? Esther wasn't very old. She was a young Jewish girl who won a beauty contest and became queen. But she was reminded that she might have become queen so God could use her to save the Jewish people in her land from being murdered.

Esther had to be courageous (she could have been killed). She had to be honest (the king didn't know she was Jewish). She had to trust God to take care of her and she asked others to pray for her. God can use you, too.

Can you be courageous, honest, and trust Him? Sure you can ... and don't forget to ask others to hold you up in prayer.

Dear God,

Help me to be courageous, honest and to trust You just like Esther.

Amen

Delighted!

Who matters more to you than anything? Do you try to be just like your friends? Dress like them? Have the same opinions as them? Like the same things? Even if you sometimes know that the things they do or think are wrong?

What delights you? That's a word you probably don't use too often. "I'm delighted to hang out at the mall with you guys!" Nah – it doesn't sound right. Stop and think about it, though.

When something delights you, it brings you pleasure. What does that mean for you? Is it being just like your friends or is it pleasing God? Do you find delight in His Word and learning how He wants you to live? I hope so ... that delights Him!

Dear God,

My friends are really important to me. But I don't want them to be more important than You. Help me take delight in Your Word. *Amen*

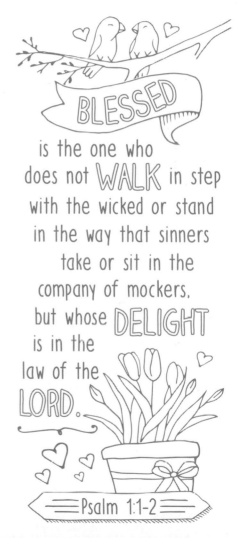

BLESSED is the one who does not **WALK** in step with the wicked or stand in the way that sinners take or sit in the company of mockers, but whose **DELIGHT** is in the law of the **LORD.**

Psalm 1:1-2

Respect God

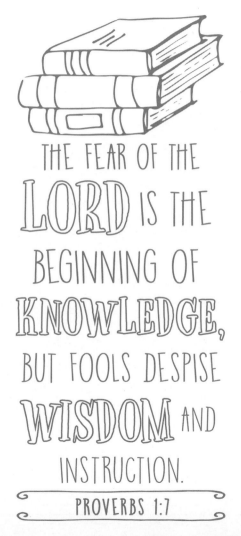

THE FEAR OF THE **LORD** IS THE BEGINNING OF **KNOWLEDGE,** BUT FOOLS DESPISE **WISDOM** AND INSTRUCTION.

PROVERBS 1:7

*T*hink you're pretty smart, do ya? Do you even sometimes brag that you aren't scared of *anything*? Well, even if you believe that's true, it may not be a good thing.

Fear of the Lord is where smarts begins. Now this doesn't mean so much fear, like fear of the dark or fear of spiders. It means a healthy full-blooded *respect*. When you begin to understand God's power and that He absolutely will not tolerate sin, especially deliberate sin, then you begin to respect who He is.

That's when your knowledge begins. Part of that respect is understanding that God will discipline you sometimes, just as your parents do. He cares about you and wants you to learn and grow in your faith.

Dear Father,

Help me to be smart. Help me learn to respect You and to grow. Thanks for caring. *Amen*

Plan of Love

A plan. That's what God has had since the beginning of time. Nothing – not one thing – has happened that has surprised Him. He has probably been disappointed a few times, but not surprised. He knew the choice Adam and Eve would make. He knew every time that the Israelites would complain about stuff.

He knows when you're going to choose to turn away from Him rather than obey Him. He knows ... and He loves you anyway. In fact, He loved mankind so much that He sent His Son to teach people how to live. Then He died and rose back to life so that anyone who believes in Him can one day go to heaven. That's quite a plan. A plan based on love.

Dear Lord,

Thank You that from the very beginning You have had a loving plan for mankind and for me.

Amen

For to us a child is born, to us a son is given, and the government will be on His shoulders. And He will be called Wonderful Counselor, Mighty God, Everlasting Father, Prince of Peace.

Isaiah 9:6

Stuck like Glue

You will keep in perfect **PEACE** those whose **MINDS** are **STEADFAST**, because they **TRUST IN YOU.**

Isaiah 26:3

What image pops into your mind when you think about peace? A quiet lake reflecting the mountains around it? A dove silently flying across the sky? A baby quietly sleeping? Is your life quiet and peaceful like that? Do you want it to be? How do you get it?

This little verse in Isaiah has the answer – keep your mind and heart on God. Don't just think about Him once in a while, settle your mind into a pattern of thinking about Him. Keep your mind stuck on Him – like glue. The more you think about Him, read His Word, talk to Him, the better you will know Him and the more you will trust Him.

So, there you go – sticking like glue to God leads to trusting Him which leads to peace. Simple.

Dear God,

I want peace in my life. Please help me to learn to settle my mind on You. Help me learn to trust You so I can find real peace. Amen

Fiery Faith

Throw out your faith in God or be thrown into a white hot fire!" There's no halfway ... there is only *no God* or *fire*! Shadrach, Meshach and Abednego had to make that choice and they chose God. Each of those young men loved God so much that they were ready to die for their faith.

Amazing ... do you love *anything* enough that you would be willing to die for it? Well, God honored their faith. He protected them in the fiery furnace – no, He didn't just protect them, He sent His angel to walk in the fire with them!

The king who threw them in there in the first place was so impressed that he began praising God. God honors faith. Lives are changed by active faith.

Dear God,

Those guys were brave! Help me to learn to have that kind of faith. I love You now. I want to love You more!

Amen

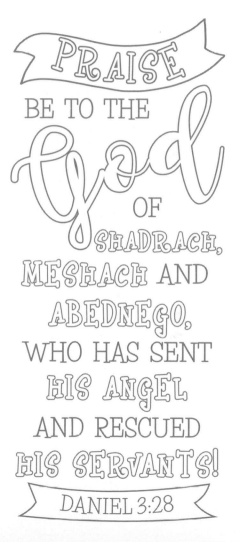

PRAISE BE TO THE God OF SHADRACH, MESHACH AND ABEDNEGO, WHO HAS SENT HIS ANGEL AND RESCUED HIS SERVANTS! DANIEL 3:28

The Best Choice

THE **LORD PROVIDED** A **HUGE FISH** TO SWALLOW **JONAH,** AND JONAH WAS IN THE BELLY OF THE **FISH** THREE DAYS AND THREE NIGHTS.

JONAH 1:17

So ... how about the whole "obeying" thing? Does it seem like there is *always* someone telling you what to do? When the things you're told to do are things you *do not* want to do, then it's even stinkier! Jonah knew about that. God told him to warn the people in Nineveh to clean up their act.

Jonah didn't want to. So, he took off in the opposite direction. Apparently he thought God wouldn't know where he was. *Wrong.*

The bottom line is that Jonah ended up in the belly of a fish for three days and nights to think about his disobedience. He decided it was better to obey and God gave him another chance when the fish kind of, umm, threw him up. So ... obey God. It's the best choice.

Dear God,

Obeying is hard sometimes. But help me to remember that it's important to obey ... especially You.   *Amen*

Devoted to God

Fill a glass to the top with water. Can you fill that same glass with milk? Of course not, it's already full of water. It can't be filled with two things.

Your heart can't be full of two things either. When there are two things shouting for your attention and energy, you will end up resenting one of them. Some people pour love for money into their hearts instead of love for God.

Money can't be the most important thing in your life. God wants to be most important and He will not share the number one spot with anything else. Be devoted to God alone.

Dear God,

It's so tempting to want more and more money. But I don't want anything to be more important to me than You are. Help me to be filled with You and You alone. *Amen*

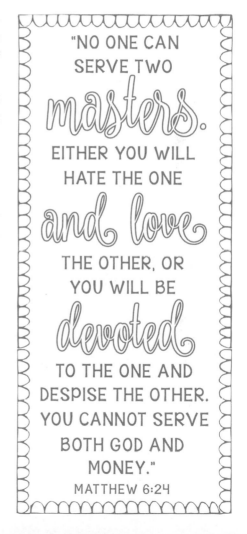

"NO ONE CAN SERVE TWO *masters.* EITHER YOU WILL HATE THE ONE *and love* THE OTHER, OR YOU WILL BE *devoted* TO THE ONE AND DESPISE THE OTHER. YOU CANNOT SERVE BOTH GOD AND MONEY."
MATTHEW 6:24

Good Gifts

"If you, then, though you are evil, know how to give **GOOD GIFTS** to your children, how much more will **YOUR FATHER** in **HEAVEN** give good gifts to those who **ASK HIM!**"

Matthew 7:11

God wants to give you good things. Think about that ... the Creator of the universe *wants* to give you good things. Even more than your own mom and dad want to give you stuff. He loves you that much.

"Well, okay," you say. "Bring it on, God. Give me all you want!" Hold on there – what God wants to give you may not be "stuff" like phones or designer clothes.

He wants to give you things that will grow your faith in Him and your sensitivity to other people. He wants to make you a better person. He cares that much!

Dear God,

It blows me away that You love me that much! Thank You for every gift You have already given me. Help me to become the woman You want me to be.

Amen

Real Love

*I*t may not feel like it sometimes, but your parents love you – a lot! Most parents would do anything to protect their children from any kind of pain. The average mom or dad would never set their child up to be hurt at all.

But, God did. He had one Son ... one. No other kids at home to help ease the pain. He sent His one Son, Jesus, away from home (heaven) to live on earth. He taught people how to treat each other and how to worship God. Some of them responded by torturing and killing Him and God allowed it to happen ... because of His love for those very people.

You are a part of those people. God did it for mankind. He loves us that much.

Dear God,

It must have hurt You to see what Jesus went through. Thank You for loving me that much.

Amen

FOR God SO loved THE WORLD, THAT HE GAVE HIS ONLY SON, THAT WHOEVER *believes* IN *Him* SHOULD NOT PERISH BUT HAVE *eternal life.*

JOHN 3:16

Bread and Water

"I AM THE BREAD OF LIFE."

JOHN 6:35

*B*read and water are not exactly gourmet foods. But bread and water are staples of a good diet. A person can live for a long time on bread and water. Jesus promised to be bread and water for His children.

In the rest of this verse, He isn't saying that your stomach will never growl or you will never have a cotton mouth. He is saying that your soul will never be hungry or thirsty again if you come to Him. He is all you need.

Jesus will fill you with His love. He will care for you and protect you. He will guide you and teach you. You need nothing else but Him.

Dear God,

This is so hard to understand 'cause it seems like there are so many things that I need. Help me to understand how Jesus can be everything to me. I want to learn that. *Amen*

Never Alone

Saying goodbye stinks! Have you ever had to say goodbye to a friend who moved away? What about a brokenhearted goodbye to a boyfriend? A real heart-wrenching goodbye is never easy!

Jesus knew He was going to die. He knew that His leaving was not going to be easy for His friends. After all, He had spent pretty much every minute for 3½ years with them. They would miss Him.

So He asked His Father to send someone to be with them. That was the Holy Spirit. Jesus cared about His friends so much that He didn't want them to be alone. He wanted them to always know His presence and to keep learning and growing in their faith.

Dear Father,

Thank You that Jesus cared so much. Thank You that You care that much, too. I know the Holy Spirit is always with me. *Amen*

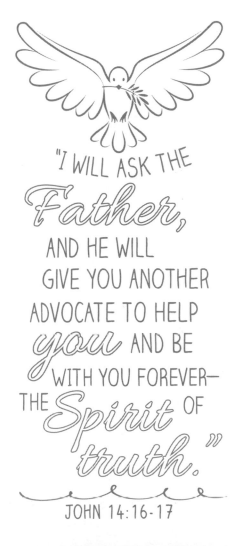

"I WILL ASK THE *Father,* AND HE WILL GIVE YOU ANOTHER ADVOCATE TO HELP *you* AND BE WITH YOU FOREVER— THE *Spirit* OF *truth.*"

JOHN 14:16-17

Copycat

Walk in love, ♡ as Christ loved us and gave Himself up for us.

Ephesians 5:2

Okay, be honest. Do you and your friends buy the same style and brand of clothes? Do you like to do the same things? Seriously ... aren't you kind of imitators of whatever style is really hot right now?

Jesus gave a standard to copy. He said everyone should imitate God – be a copycat of God. He even explained what that means. Imitating God means loving other people. A life of love means loving – not just when you feel like it.

Loving your friends who are a lot like you, now that's easy. A life of love means loving those who are different from you. It means loving when it isn't easy. To love like that, you have to be close to God – you must copy Him!

Dear Father,

Help me to learn to love like that. It isn't easy to love kids who are different from me and my friends. Help me love like You do. *Amen*

Disciplined in Love

Discipline ... is not fun. Being grounded or punished by having privileges taken away stinks. Did you ever think about the fact that your parents don't enjoy punishing you? However, discipline is necessary. It keeps you from doing wrong things. Parents have to discipline you, but it makes them sad to make you sad.

God's discipline is very similar. He disciplines you because He loves you. But He doesn't enjoy making you sad or angry. He just knows that if you aren't disciplined you will continue going down a wrong path. You won't learn the right way. Discipline means you are loved.

Dear God,

Well, I don't like being disciplined. It isn't fun and it means that I've messed up. But, well, I'm glad You love me enough to discipline me.

Amen

THE LORD ♡ DISCIPLINES ♡ THE ONE HE LOVES.

HEBREWS 12:6

Walking in the Light

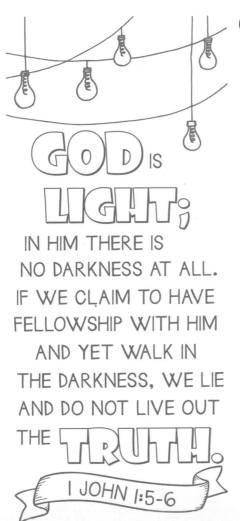

GOD IS **LIGHT;** IN HIM THERE IS NO DARKNESS AT ALL. IF WE CLAIM TO HAVE FELLOWSHIP WITH HIM AND YET WALK IN THE DARKNESS, WE LIE AND DO NOT LIVE OUT THE **TRUTH.**

I JOHN 1:5-6

Do you know the old saying, "You can't judge a book by its cover"? It means that the artwork on the cover may promise one thing, but inside the plot is totally different.

The same thing holds true of your walk with God. You can make all the claims you want about how much you pray and how often you read the Bible and how close you are to God ... but you can't fool God. What's truly in your heart will be evident to God – selfishness, a mean spirit, anger, a lack of love.

If those things are living in your heart, then you can make all the claims you want about how much you are living for God. He will know the truth and the truth will be that you have been lying.

Dear God,

I don't want to live a lie. Help me to really walk in the light ... Your light. Amen

Time to Pray

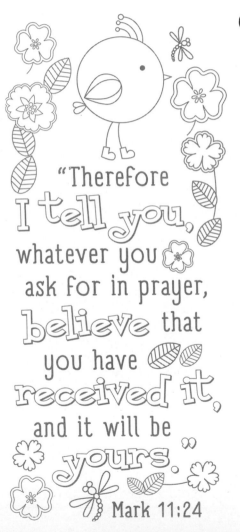

"Therefore I tell you, whatever you ask for in prayer, believe that you have received it, and it will be yours."

Mark 11:24

"Dear God, please help ... y-a-w-n ... blah, blah, blah ..." Does that kinda sound like your prayers? When you pray, do you believe God hears you? Do you believe He cares? Do you believe He might actually answer your prayers? If you don't, then you're just praying because you think that's what you're supposed to do. Or, maybe you're hoping that God just might actually hear you and answer.

That's not the way the Bible says to pray. Jesus spoke these words in Mark 11 and He said that when you pray you should believe God hears you and that He will answer. That, my friend, is a command from the top!

Dear God,

Knowing You actually hear my prayers changes how I'm going to pray. I know now that prayer can make a difference. Amen

Thankful All the Time

"Okay," you may say, "I've heard this praying all the time stuff before. But, giving thanks in all circumstances ... really? Does it really mean *all* circumstances, even the bad?"

Let's get real here. Is the Bible telling you to jump with joy when a loved one dies? What about if your friends start acting goofy and stop being friends with you? Well, yeah, that is what this verse says. But does God expect you to be *thankful* for rotten things that happen? No, but you *can* be thankful that you don't have to go through any of that stuff by yourself.

God knows everything that's going on. He will help you, strengthen you and never leave you alone. You can thank Him continually for that.

Dear God,

Thank You that You are always with me. Thank You for sticking close and giving me strength when things get rough. That helps. *Amen*

Pray continually, give thanks in all circumstances; for this is God's will for you in Christ Jesus.

I Thessalonians 5:17-18

Make it Right

From inside the *fish* Jonah prayed to the *Lord* his *God.*

Jonah 2:1

Have you ever messed up so bad that you thought things were hopeless? Well, you'd think that if anyone was going to be that low it would be Jonah. After all, he had disobeyed God, run away from Him, hidden in a boat and then ended up being swallowed by a fish.

But, as bad as things were, Jonah turned to God. He didn't wait to get to a nice, clean church to pray and ask God's forgiveness. Right there in the belly of the great fish, Jonah turned to God, confessed his sin and asked forgiveness. When you know you've messed up, get it straightened out with God. He will hear your prayer from wherever you are. He will forgive you and help you get back on track.

Dear God,

Help me to remember that I can pray anytime, anywhere and You will hear me. *Amen*

Frontline Prayer

Simple, huh? Trust God and He will answer your prayers. It might surprise you to know that this little nine-word sentence comes in the middle of the description of a terrible battle. Some soldiers cried out to God in the middle of a battle and He answered their prayers and helped them win.

The key here, though, is that these men trusted that God would hear their prayer and that He would answer. God rewarded their trust.

How much trust is involved in your prayers? It's easy to pray fancy prayers when things are going great. But, when you're in the middle of a battle, do you believe He hears your prayer? You should – His track record recorded in the Bible shows how much He cares.

Dear God,

I don't know why it's so hard for me to trust You. Help me learn how to trust.

Amen

HE ANSWERED THEIR prayers, BECAUSE THEY trusted IN Him.

1 Chronicles 5:20

Pray for Peace

"PRAY for those who mistreat you."

Luke 6:28

*W*HAT? Pray for the creeps who push me around, make fun of me and generally make life miserable? *No way!* Oh wait, maybe I will pray for them – pray that their hair falls out and they each get a zillion pimples – the kind that really hurts! Umm, no, that won't work.

When Jesus said to pray for those who mistreat you, He meant to really pray for them. Prayer is conversation with God. Talking with God means your heart lines up with His and God's heart is filled with love. You can't continue to be angry with someone you are praying for. So, praying for your enemies leads to peace in your own heart. Not a bad side benefit, eh?

Dear God,

Help me to be strong enough to pray for my enemies. I can't do it without Your help.

Amen

Never Alone

"Hey, a little help here!" Ever feel like you're walking in complete darkness? So dark that you can't even see your hand in front of your face? You cry out for help but your words seem to bounce right back into your face. You feel alone. All alone.

Maybe you're crying out to the wrong people. Maybe you're looking for help in the wrong places. God will hear your prayers. He will teach you how to live and He will show you what His will is. He has promised that His Holy Spirit will lead you. You're not alone. God wants to help you. He's just waiting for you to ask. Go on ... ask.

Dear God,

I need Your help. Just like the psalmist, I am asking You to help me and teach me. Thank You for never leaving me alone. *Amen*

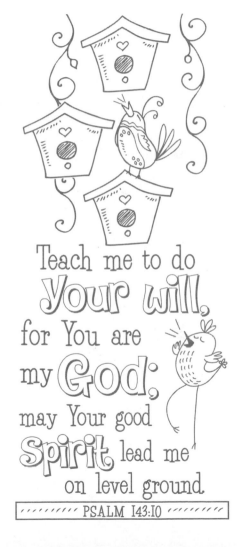

Teach me to do Your will, for You are my God; may Your good Spirit lead me on level ground.

PSALM 143:10

No Worries

Do not be anxious about anything, but in EVERYTHING, by PRAYER & supplication with thanksgiving let your requests be made known to GOD.

Philippians 4:6

Cold sweat breaks out on your forehead. Breath comes in short, shallow gasps. Your senses are heightened so much that you think you can hear a pin hit the floor. You are ready to run at a moment's notice. What's going on? Fear – simple, heart-pounding fear. What makes you afraid? What makes you worry? What do you do with all of those emotions?

God says you should bring them to Him. After all, when you think about it, He's the only One who can actually do something about the things that worry or scare You. Trust Him enough to bring those things to Him. Don't worry ... pray!

Dear God,

I waste a lot of energy worrying or being scared when all I really need to do is bring my fears to You. Thank You for caring. Help me to remember to come to You first ... then I won't need to worry later.

Amen

Number One

Have you ever wanted something so much that you could almost taste it? So much that you couldn't think about anything else? That thing you wanted so badly or the attention of someone you cared about and craved colored everything else.

Well, you can almost hear the longing in God's voice in this verse. He wants His people to turn to Him. God wants your love. He wants you to put aside your pride ... your own agenda ... to humble yourself before Him. He wants to be most important. He wants to forgive your sin.

All He asks is humbleness and prayer.

Dear God,

I know that sometimes I'm more important to me than You are. Help me to learn to get myself out of the way and seek Your will. *Amen*

"IF MY PEOPLE, who are called by MY NAME, will HUMBLE themselves and pray and seek MY FACE and TURN FROM their wicked ways, then I will hear from HEAVEN, and I will FORGIVE THEIR sin and will HEAL THEIR LAND."

2 Chronicles 7:14

Best Prayers

"When you pray, do not be like the hypocrites, for they love to pray standing in the synagogues & on the street corners to be seen by others."

Matthew 6:5

Show-offs, don't you hate 'em? People who always have to be the center of attention. No matter what's going on, they get louder and goofier so that everyone looks at them. They think they are so cool.

Is it hard to believe that some people actually show off when they are praying? Yeah, they pray long and loud and use fancy words. It "sounds" like they are super-spiritual. But what's in their hearts is not so pure. They are putting on a show for people ... it is not for God.

When you pray, don't put on a show for others, remember that you don't have to say fancy words and pray long prayers. Just pray what's in your heart.

Dear God,

I love You. I want to pray what's in my heart and be honest with You. Thanks for hearing my prayers.

Amen

Make a Difference

"I can't do anything, I'm just a kid. Nothing I say or do makes any difference to anyone." Is that what you think? Well, hold on there Miss Negative! It just isn't so. This verse promises that your prayers can make a difference in your life and the lives of others.

If your heart really desires to serve God – if it's righteous – your prayers make a difference. Don't view the "righteous" part of this as a negative. It doesn't mean you don't ever sin or do something wrong. It means that in the center of your heart you truly desire to serve and obey God. He knows you're going to mess up sometimes. He doesn't expect perfection – it's not possible anyway. Keep your heart focused on God and pray for all you're worth – it makes a difference.

Dear God,

Thank You that I can make a difference by praying. We're quite a team. *Amen*

JAMES 5:16
THE PRAYER OF A RIGHTEOUS PERSON HAS GREAT POWER AS IT IS WORKING.

Good Things

Praise the LORD, for the LORD is good, SING to His name, for it is PLEASANT!

♪♫ Psalm 135:3 ♪

Hey, when someone starts saying nice things about you, do you tell them to stop or do you eat it up? It makes you feel good to hear nice things about yourself. It's nice to know you are appreciated and that people see your good qualities or your efforts to do nice things.

Good reminder – don't make all your prayers, "God, do this or help that or give me." Take time every day to thank God for what He does for you. Praise Him for His loving kindness, for giving you your family, friends, home. Praise Him for the world He created. Praise Him for taking care of you. Praise Him for having a plan for your life. Praise Him every day.

Dear God,

I am so sorry that my prayers are so often "Give me ..." I do praise You for Your love and care.

Amen

Prayer Partners

Go without food for three days ... yeah, right ... and do what? Well, usually fasting is associated with praying. So, when Queen Esther asked Mordecai to have the Jews fast for her, she probably assumed they were praying for her, too. It worked and God helped her protect the Jewish people from being killed.

Queen Esther was smart – she knew she needed prayer support. She had a job to do that was too big to do alone. Most jobs are.

Everyone needs the prayers of others to help them through life. Talk to someone you trust about being your prayer partner. Share things with each other and pray for each other.

Dear God,

Help me to find a good prayer partner ... someone who will pray with me about things.

Amen

Go, gather together all the Jews who are in Susa, & **FAST** for me. Do not **EAT** or **DRINK** for three days, night or day. I and my attendants will fast as you do.

Esther 4:16

Prayer and Praise

ABOUT MIDNIGHT Paul & Silas WERE praying & SINGING HYMNS TO GOD, AND THE OTHER PRISONERS WERE LISTENING TO THEM.

ACTS 16:25

How nice. Paul and Silas had a prison ministry – visiting the prisoners and having a praise and worship time for them. *Not quite!* Paul and Silas *were* prisoners. Their feet were in chains. They couldn't get up and walk around. They hadn't done anything wrong. They just preached about God and were thrown into prison.

Why on earth were they praying and singing when they were in prison? They knew that prayer and praise are not just for when things are going great. They had an audience of prisoners who needed to know that God loved them. Paul and Silas didn't waste time feeling sorry for themselves. How do you react when life gets stinky? Do you complain or pray? Remember that others are listening to you.

Dear God,

I forgot that others are listening. Help me to act like Paul and Silas.

Amen

Let Go

...Casting ALL YOUR ANXIETIES ON Him, BECAUSE He cares FOR YOU.

1 PETER 5:7

*W*hat kinds of things do you worry about? What keeps you awake at night with a knot in your stomach? Stop and think about it – does any of the stuff you worry about actually happen? Most of it doesn't, so why spend so much time worrying? It's easy to simply say ... *stop worrying.* But it's hard to let it go 'cause you have to have somewhere to put that energy.

The best thing to do is to put that energy into prayer. Give your problems and worries to God. He cares about what worries you and He can take care of it. Just give it to Him.

Dear God,

It's hard to let go of the things that worry or scare me. Help me to be able to give those things to You and just leave them there.

Amen

Just Ask

> "Ask and it will be given to you; seek and you will find; knock and the door will be ❀ ❀ opened to you. For everyone who asks receives; the one who seeks finds; & to the one who knocks, the door will be opened."
>
> MATTHEW 7:7-8

When someone makes a promise to you, do you absolutely believe that they will keep that promise? Do you plan on it and start living as if it's already done? Some people aren't so good at keeping promises or maybe they keep a promise half way. But you can plan on God's promises.

These words in Matthew were spoken by Jesus. Sounds like there's a whole lot of stuff that people don't have just because they don't ask for it. God wants to give you so much because He loves you. Line your heart up with Him and ask for His blessings and guidance in life.

Dear God,

I don't want to miss stuff just because I didn't ask. Please help me to keep asking You for guidance and help. Amen

Wait, Wait, Wait!

*W*aiting is not fun! Are you a patient waiter who goes quietly about life until the things happen you've been waiting for? How about with God? Do you ask God to do something or help with something, then get tired of waiting and take matters into your own hands?

Here's a news flash – you can't take care of things as well as He can. The psalmist learned that it was important to wait patiently for God. David cried out to God then waited and God heard his prayers.

Waiting is not fun. It's not easy. But, when you wait, you have time to learn to trust God and to think about if you really want Him to do what you asked in the heat of the moment.

Dear God,

I'm too impatient. Help me to be more patient. Help me to learn to trust You more. *Amen*

I waited

patiently for the

LORD;

He turned

to me and heard my cry.

Psalm 40:1

Needs vs. Wants

MY GOD WILL SUPPLY *every* NEED OF YOURS ACCORDING TO HIS RICHES IN *glory* IN CHRIST JESUS.

PHILIPPIANS 4:19

*D*oes this sound familiar ... "I need new shoes," or "I need an iPad," or "I need a new phone?" Now, stop and think about how many times you tell your parents you *need* something. Do you really need those things or do you simply *want* them? Are your prayers want-based instead of need-based? Often we try to tell God what to do because we want our lives to be easier or happier. We ask Him to do things the way we *want*.

God hasn't promised to do that. He promised to supply our needs. That's a whole different thing. Think about it — has God supplied your needs? Most likely. Stop and thank Him for knowing what's best for you and supplying those things.

Dear God,

This is hard. Thank You for supplying my needs and for understanding when I pray for what I want. *Amen*

Forgive and Forget

Hey ... who do you think you are? Do you really think it's okay to talk to God – telling Him how sorry you are for the wrong things you've done and asking Him to forgive you when you're holding anger in your heart toward someone? Get real. If you dare to ask God to forgive your sins, you'd better be willing to forgive others for whatever they have done.

There's an old saying that says what's good for the goose is good for the gander – yeah, strange, but what it means is that if God is kind and forgiving enough to forgive you, then you should certainly forgive others. Come to God with a pure heart so He can forgive you and bless you.

Dear God,

I guess that makes sense. Help me be forgiving of others. Actually, I'll be glad to get rid of the anger anyway. It takes a lot of energy to hold a grudge.

Amen

"When you stand PRAYING, if you hold anything against anyone, FORGIVE THEM, so that your FATHER in heaven may forgive you your sins." Mark 11:25

Strength and Courage

WHEN I called, YOU ANSWERED ME; You greatly EMBOLDENED ME.

PSALM 138:3

Ever feel like you're on your own? Like no one understands you? And no one can really do anything about the junk in your life anyway. Maybe you turn to your friends or a boyfriend for help ... and they can't do anything. The bottom line is even the people who love you can't fix the problems in your life. That job is God's and God's alone. Call on Him. Ask Him to give you courage and wisdom. Ask Him to walk with you through life. He will. He promised.

The psalmist found that out. God answered his cry and made him strong and courageous. You can handle a lot in life when you know you aren't alone!

Dear God,

Thank You for hearing my prayers. Help me find strength and courage in knowing that I'm not alone.

Amen

Adoration

Who is your favorite singing group? Have you ever gone to one of their concerts? Did the crowd shout and scream? Do you have posters of the singer up in your room? Do you try to dress like them, wear your hair like them? Do you admire everything they say and do? Know what? Only God is worthy of being adored like that.

That's a part of prayer that just can't be ignored – adoring God for who He is and for all He does for you. Stop and think about the stories in the Bible of God's care for His people. Think about the miracles He did to protect them.

Look around at the beautiful world He made. Remember that He thought of families, friends, pets ... all the things that fill your life with joy. Adore Him for His creativity and generosity.

Dear God,

I do adore You. Thank You for all You have done for me and given me.

Amen

GIVE THANKS TO THE LORD, FOR HE IS GOOD. HIS LOVE ENDURES FOREVER.

PSALM 136:1

Confession Is Good

If we confess our sins, HE IS FAITHFUL & just to FORGIVE us our sins.
1 John 1:9

When you get the order to clean your room from your mom, do you ever just stuff a bunch of junk under the bed or in your closet so the floor looks clean? Do you ever throw clean clothes into the laundry hamper instead of hanging them up?

Yeah, covering up stuff is not the same as cleaning. The same is true with prayer. God says you should confess your sin – admit what you've done wrong. Don't try to cover it up, just confess. When you do, He promises to forgive you and cleanse you. That's a good trade-off for honesty, right?

Dear God,

It's hard to admit that I've done wrong things. I guess I think that if I don't admit it, maybe You won't notice. That is the wrong way to think. Okay, I'm sorry for my sin. Please forgive me.

Amen

Teamwork!

A basketball or soccer team only wins games if all the players work together. If there's a superstar who doesn't help his teammates or pass the ball to them, then the team won't win many games. Teammates need each other. God's children need each other, too. That's why the Bible tells us to pray for each other. Your prayers for other Christians will help them be strong and stay close to God.

Your prayers will help you feel close to others, too – you'll feel like a teammate as you hold your friends and family members up in prayer before God. You'll also feel like you have a part in their walk with God. Pray for others – all the time!

Dear God,

I need others' prayers and I want to remember to pray for others. Thanks for the team!

Amen

Be *alert* and always keep on *praying* for all the *Lord's* people.

Ephesians 6:18

Prayer Helper

He who searches OUR hearts knows the mind of the SPIRIT, because the Spirit intercedes for GOD'S people in accordance with the will of GOD. Romans 8:27

No doubt you believe prayer is important. After all, you've probably heard about prayer ever since you started going to church or Sunday school. But, have you ever been in a place where the problems in your life are so overwhelming that you just don't know what to pray – you can't find the words to make sense of what you're feeling?

Not to worry. Remember that Jesus asked God to send the Holy Spirit to always be with believers. Well, the Holy Spirit doesn't just hang out with you – He prays for you! When You can't find the words to say what's in your heart, the Holy Spirit will pray for you! He knows exactly what you need.

Dear God,

Thank You so much for the Holy Spirit. Thank You for His prayers for me. I'm thankful for His help.

Amen

World Leaders

Did you know that you can play a part in world decisions? Yeah, presidents, senators, representatives, kings, prime ministers ... people who make decisions that affect the whole world need your prayers. Do you think to pray for them?

These verses encourage you to pray for those in authority. After all, they need God a lot! They make decisions about wars, taxes and normal every-day life for everyone. When you pray for God to lead and guide them, that puts you on their team and that gives you a part in their work.

Remember to pray for these world leaders to follow God and to lead their nations with the wisdom He gives.

I URGE, THEN, FIRST OF ALL, THAT PETITIONS, PRAYERS, INTERCESSION AND THANKSGIVING BE MADE FOR ALL PEOPLE—FOR KINGS AND ALL THOSE IN AUTHORITY, THAT WE MAY LIVE PEACEFUL & QUIET LIVES.

I TIMOTHY 2:1-2

Dear God,

Wow! I didn't realize how important my prayers could be. I pray that the leaders of my country will follow You closely. *Amen*

Best News Ever

PRAY FOR US that the MESSAGE of the LORD may SPREAD RAPIDLY and be honored, just as it was WITH YOU.

2 Thessalonians 3:1

When you hear some really good news, what's the first thing you do? Probably hop on the phone and call a friend to tell her the good news, right? What kinds of things do you and your friends talk about? News about other people; about singing groups; about school? News about those kinds of things spreads pretty quickly.

But the most important news in the world; the most important news in all of history should be the quickest spreading news – the news of God's love. Remember to pray for people who have made it their life's work to share that good news. Pray for the message to spread around the world. It's the most important message ever!

Dear God,

Help missionaries around the world do their work to tell people about You. Help my minister, too, as he works right here in our town.

Amen

Praise God!

Yahoo for God! Praise God all the time. Praise God everywhere. Praise Him with every breath. Forget about asking God for stuff. Forget about complaining. Just stop and praise Him.

Let your mind and heart fill up with thoughts of how loving and kind He is. Think about His power. Think about His creativity and His gifts to you.

Dance around and sing a joyful song of praise to Him. Go ahead – you'll enjoy it – and so will God!

Dear God,

I praise You for mountains and oceans. I praise You for flowers, butterflies, puppies and kittens. I praise You for my family and my friends. I praise You for loving me and taking care of me. I praise You for everything!

Amen

PRAISE the LORD.
PRAISE GOD ♪
in His sanctuary...
PRAISE
HIM for His
acts of power...
PRAISE HIM
with the sounding
of the trumpet...
let everything that
HAS BREATH
PRAISE the LORD.
♪ Psalm 150:1-3, 5 ♪

Daily Bread

"GIVE US EACH DAY OUR DAILY BREAD."

LUKE 11:3

Some people never have enough of anything. They want more money, a bigger house, a nicer car ... what about you? Are you always wanting more clothes, more CDs ... more stuff? When do you have enough?

Jesus taught an example of how to pray. It's known as the Lord's Prayer. He taught us to pray for our daily bread – what we *need* for each day. That's all. His prayer example reminds us that some people don't have enough food to eat for one day, but others store food up so they have supplies for months and months. Some people pray for just a piece of bread for today while others have fancy houses, cars and so much stuff that ... well, it's embarrassing. Pray for what you *need*, not for excess. And, thank God for what He gives you.

Dear God,

Thank You for giving me food for each day. Thank You for all You give me. *Amen*

Cleaned Up

"FORGIVE US OUR SINS, FOR WE ALSO FORGIVE EVERYONE WHO SINS AGAINST US."

LUKE 11:4

Say it's a hot summer's day and you've been out playing soccer. You're dirty, sweaty and your hair is messy. Then, it's time to go to a friend's birthday party. Do you just go in your dirty, sweaty condition? Of course not; you take a shower, wash your hair and put on clean clothes. You get cleaned up.

Getting cleaned up is part of a healthy prayer life, too. When you pray, don't immediately hit God with a lot of "gimmes and do this stuff," get cleaned up first. Confess your sins and ask His forgiveness. Clean up your whole heart by forgiving people you've been holding a grudge against. Once you're cleaned up, you can praise Him and bring your requests to Him.

Dear God,

Help me to remember to get cleaned up and repent at the beginning of my talks with You.

Amen

Mountain Movers

"IF YOU HAVE **FAITH** AND DO NOT DOUBT...YOU CAN SAY TO THIS **MOUNTAIN,** 'GO, THROW YOURSELF INTO THE **SEA,'** AND IT WILL BE DONE."

MATTHEW 21:21

Do you believe you can lift a 500 lb weight with one hand? Yeah, you probably *don't* believe that your one arm has that much strength. Well, how about your prayers. Do you believe that your prayers have any power at all? Maybe you don't bother to pray for things that seem impossible because you just don't believe God can do what you want or that He will do what you want.

What's amazing is that there is so much power available to us if we just believe! Think about it – you could move a mountain if you really had faith and didn't doubt. Try it!

Dear God,

I want to make a difference in the world. Help my faith to grow. Help me to believe that You hear my prayers and that You will answer!

Amen

An Undivided Heart

Do you know someone who is "best friends" with you when you're together, but when you're not, she talks about you to others? That stinks, doesn't it?

Well, imagine how God feels when His children have a divided heart. One minute they're praising Him and asking His help with stuff, but the next minute they're trashing somebody or using God's name as a swear word, or being unkind or stealing ... anything that is the opposite of walking in the truth.

Don't be guilty of a divided heart. Ask God to teach you to walk in His ways and to keep your heart on track.

Dear God,

Sometimes my heart is divided. Sometimes I live for You and sometimes I don't. Teach me how to always live for You and to keep my heart focused on You.

Amen

TEACH ME **your way, Lord,** THAT I MAY RELY ON YOUR FAITHFULNESS; GIVE ME AN UNDIVIDED **heart,** THAT I MAY FEAR **YOUR NAME.**

PSALM 86:11

First Call

Is anyone among you in trouble? Let them pray. Is anyone happy? Let them sing songs of praise.

James 5:13

Honesty time – where do you go when you're in trouble? Do you call a friend or text message her? Do you spill your guts and cry and try to figure out an answer with her? You're going to the wrong place. God is where your help is. When you've got troubles, take them to Him. He cares and He can see the big picture of how this problem might make you stronger. He won't let your troubles kill you. But He will let you learn from them.

Also, when you're happy and things are going great, remember to praise Him. The bottom line is – talk to God every day, about everything!

Dear God,

Sometimes talking to You isn't my first thought. It might even be my fourth or fifth thought. I'm sorry. I know You love me and care about what's happening. I'll come to You first – when I need help and when I'm happy!

Amen

Single-Minded

"Anyone who loves Me will obey My teaching."
John 14:23

*L*ook at the front and the back of a piece of paper. Now, separate the front from the back. What? You can't? Of course not, the front and back sides may be different – have different things written on them – but they are part of the same piece of paper. They cannot be separated.

To what do you owe this amazing science lesson? Just this ... if you claim to love God but secretly disobey His teachings ... you're living a lie. A person who claims to love God will obey Him.

That cannot be separated out of life. Of course, everyone stumbles sometimes and everyone sins, but if the true desire of your heart is to obey God ... well, you're like that piece of paper – front and back for God!

Dear God,

I want to be better at obeying. Please help me.

Amen

No Other Gods

"You shall have no other gods BEFORE ME."

Exodus 20:3

*L*et's begin at the beginning. The first commandment God gave is that He wants to be Number One in your life. He won't share that place with anyone or anything else.

So, the first step in obeying God is to make Him more important in your life than friends or stuff! You can't serve God *and* anything else.

You can say God is most important and make your friends and family believe you mean it. You might even convince yourself that you mean it – but you can't fool God. He sees your heart so He knows what else you're concentrating on. Ask for His help in clearing other things out of your heart.

Dear God,

Whew! This is hard. Show me what else I'm allowing to be important in my heart. Show me how to push it aside so You are Number One!

Amen

No Idols

> "YOU SHALL NOT MAKE FOR YOURSELF AN IMAGE IN THE FORM OF ANYTHING IN HEAVEN ABOVE OR ON THE EARTH BENEATH OR IN THE WATERS BELOW."
>
> EXODUS 20:4

If you are a Christian that means you have asked Jesus to live in your heart. He does that in the form of the Holy Spirit – His gift to us when He went back to heaven.

Since the Spirit lives in your heart, there's no need to make any kind of statue or image and worship it.

Of course, our churches have crosses and other images that remind us of what God has done for us – but we don't worship those images.

Don't let anything bring God down to a "human" size. He's bigger than all of us, bigger than the world, bigger than the universe!

Dear God,

I don't think I make an idol of anything. But, if I do, tell me. I want You to be all I worship!

Amen

Keep God's Name Holy

How many times a day do you hear someone say something like, "God, I'm tired" or "Oh, my God, that's awesome!"? Yeah, probably hundreds. God's name has become an exclamation point in our world today.

People say His name all the time without even thinking about it. They are misusing God's holy name. It's so easy to slip into the habit of using God's name that way when you hear it so often. One way of obeying God is to be careful how you speak His name. Use His name to praise Him, to call on Him and to speak with Him. Don't use it to declare how you're feeling or anything else.

Dear God,

I hear people say Your name like that all the time. Sometimes I even slip and say it that way – or think it. I'm sorry. I want to honor Your holy name and never misuse it.

Amen

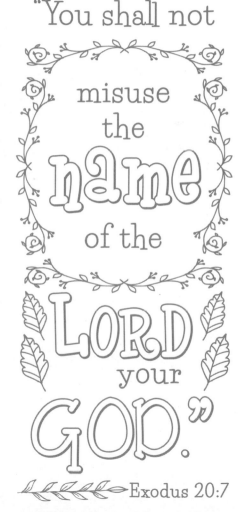

"You shall not misuse the name of the LORD your God."

Exodus 20:7

The Sabbath Day

"Remember the SABBATH DAY by keeping it HOLY."

Exodus 20:8

Sunday is the Sabbath day for our Christian faith. We call it "God's Day." We go to church and Sunday school and ... that's pretty much it. The rest of the day we pretty much do whatever we want. After going to school or working all week, we consider Saturday and Sunday to be our free days. So, we give God the two hours or so of church time and the rest of Sunday is ours. God intended that His Day be a day we spend thinking about Him, studying His Word, being with His people and honoring Him.

How can you do that? Can you spend at least some of the after-church part of His day doing something with Him or for Him? Think about it. Make a list of things you might do and get your family and friends involved, too!

Dear God,

I don't give You much time out of Your day. Give me ideas of ways to honor Your day. Amen

Honor Your Parents

"HONOR YOUR father AND YOUR mother."

EXODUS 20:12

"Hey, God – You obviously don't know my father and mother or You would never say that." Yeah, He does. He gave them to you. So, they're not perfect, neither are you. God gave you parents to teach you how to live. They take care of you, provide for you, love you and try to help you grow up to be a productive young woman. Remember, you may not always be so easy to love and live with either.

God wants you to honor your parents. That means respect them, don't talk back to them, obey the rules they lay down for you. Don't talk bad about them to your friends. Really. It will make your life so much better in the long run.

Dear God,

Sometimes my parents really make me mad. Some of their rules seem so pointless. Honoring them isn't always easy. I'm gonna need Your help for this.

Amen

Do Not Murder

"YOU SHALL not murder."

Exodus 20:13

*A*re you thinking, "Well, I'm safe on this one. I've never murdered anyone." Good – don't. But, look at this commandment in a broader way. Maybe you've never pulled a gun on someone and taken her actual life away. But what about killing someone's spirit with angry, hurtful words or a spiteful attitude?

What about crushing someone's self-image with the nasty things you say about them? Murder can take many forms. Think about the way you treat others both to their faces and behind their backs. Think about the way you treat your parents and your brothers and sisters. Whew! Maybe you don't feel so innocent anymore, huh?

Dear God,

Okay, if I think about murdering someone's self-image or their spirit – I'm not so innocent. I don't want to hurt anyone. Help me to think about the way I treat others. *Amen*

Be Faithful in Marriage

The Scripture verse for today is God's seventh commandment. When your mom and dad got married, they made a promise to love each other no matter what. It is not God's desire for married couples to separate or get divorced, and this law is important in keeping families together.

As a young girl, you can learn from this. Don't give in to peer pressure when your friends encourage you to do things that you know are wrong. Rather follow God's rules.

He made these rules for your benefit. While sometimes it may feel like you are missing out on the "fun", God gave us His commandments to ensure that we live healthy, happy lives.

Dear God,

Please help people who are married to stay true to each other, and please help me never to give in to peer pressure. *Amen*

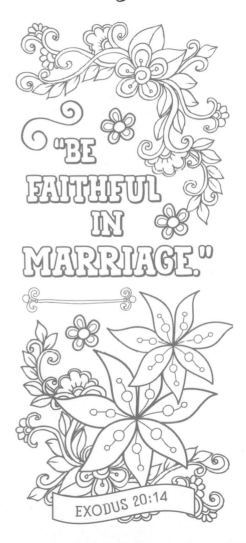

EXODUS 20:14

Don't Lie

> "YOU SHALL NOT STEAL."

EXODUS 20:15

*I*t's such a temptation sometimes, isn't it? You're in a crowded store browsing through the CDs. It would be so easy to slip one into your pocket. Who would notice? It's almost a thrill to see if you could get away with it. Some people even think they aren't guilty of stealing unless they get caught. God thinks differently.

When you take something that doesn't belong to you, the rightful owner is hurt by the loss. Stealing from a store comes back to hurt everyone in the long run because prices of products go up to pay for the stolen items.

You surely don't want anyone to steal from you – so don't steal from them. This is God's plan of how to live together in this world. Not a bad idea.

Dear God,

Stealing stinks. Please help me to never be tempted. Thanks.

Amen

Don't Steal

"You shall not give false testimony against your neighbor."

Exodus 20:16

When you say something bad about a friend, it hurts her. Gossiping, spreading rumors, criticizing – all of those things hurt. You can apologize a zillion times, but the damage is already done – even if she forgives you – because the trust is broken. It will take a long time for her to really trust your friendship again. Hurtful words lie on a person's heart like a heavy blanket.

Be careful how you talk about others. If your friends start spreading lies or half-truths about someone – put a stop to it. You can stop the rumor chain. You don't want others to spread rumors or say bad things about you, so treat them the same way.

Dear God,

When my friends and I get together sometimes we have "fun" trashing someone else. Help me to stop that kind of talk ... without making my friends mad.

Amen

Don't Covet

"You shall not covet your **neighbor's** house...or anything that **belongs** to your neighbor."

✳ ✳ ✳ ✳ ✳ ✳ ✳ ✳ ✳✳ ✳ ✳✳
✳ ✳ ✳ Exodus 20:17 ✳ ✳ ✳

*G*od knows that coveting, which means really, really wanting something that someone else has, only leads to problems.

When you can't stop thinking about that thing you will start wanting it more and more. Pretty soon you'll be jealous of the person who has that thing. Then, you'll start to dislike them. You may even end up trying to steal it and hurt the owner in the process.

Be happy with what you have. If there is something more you want, get a job, save your money and buy it for yourself. Simple, huh?

Dear God,

Some of my friends have nicer stuff than I do. It's hard not to want those things, too. But help me to stay away from coveting. I don't want my friendships to be wrecked by coveting.

Amen

Obey, Again?

Obey ... does it seem like that's all you hear? Does it sometimes seem like your parents have a zillion rules that are made just to spoil your fun? Do you ever feel like your parents have forgotten what it feels like to be a kid? You can bet they haven't.

In fact, it's probably because they do remember that they have made some of those rules. They know life is full of temptations. They know that sometimes you don't see the big picture when you make certain choices.

So, until you're more mature and can handle some of the things life throws at you, they help out with rules. Obey them without throwing a fit every time – their rules are for your own good.

Dear God,

You're going to have to help me with this. Obeying is not one of my best things. Just help me to obey without complaining. Thanks.

Amen

CHILDREN, OBEY YOUR PARENTS IN EVERYTHING, FOR THIS PLEASES THE LORD. COLOSSIANS 3:20

Lovable

"Love YOUR neighbor AS YOURSELF."

ROMANS 13:9

There just isn't any way to live a life of obedience to God if you're not loving other people. There also isn't any way to pick and choose which people to love and which people not to love.

God says to love them all. How do you love your neighbor as yourself? Well, you take care of yourself. You don't spread rumors about yourself. You do everything you can to help yourself with problems and jobs. Do those things for your neighbors.

Who, you may ask, are your neighbors? Jesus said that any person you may bump into who has a need is your neighbor – even if it's someone you've never met. Even if it's someone who is way different from you. Show that person love.

Dear God,

It's easy to love my friends and family – but some people aren't very lovable. Will You help me to love other people? Thanks. *Amen*

Bad Messages

Bombarded is exactly the right word for what the world is doing to you. It's shouting things at you about what it thinks is right.

The world yells that being intimate before marriage is okay – in fact, desirable. God says it isn't.

The world says that drugs, drinking or smoking make you cool. God says it doesn't. The world judges success by how much you have. God doesn't.

Don't get caught up in all the world's messages. Pay attention to God only – obey Him even when the world is shouting something else in your ears.

Dear God,

This is hard now and I know it's just going to get harder as I get older. Help me to pay attention to You and not the messages I get from everywhere else.

Amen

We must obey GOD rather than men.

Acts 5:29

Obedience Pays

NOAH FOUND FAVOR IN THE EYES OF THE LORD...NOAH WAS A RIGHTEOUS MAN, BLAMELESS AMONG THE PEOPLE OF HIS TIME & HE WALKED FAITHFULLY WITH GOD.

GENESIS 6:8-9

Obedience pays. It sure did in Noah's case. Noah lived for God and obeyed Him. That paid off when God got fed up with the way the rest of the people were *not* obeying Him and decided to wipe them out by sending a big flood.

Noah obeyed God, even when everyone around him didn't. They probably poked fun at Noah for his lifestyle. But, he kept on obeying. God saved Noah and his family and they were the people who had children to repopulate the earth.

So, Noah is like your great-great-great ... you get the idea ... grandfather. Anyway, don't ever think that your obedience goes unnoticed. God pays attention to that kind of stuff.

Dear God,

It's good to know that You notice that I try to live for You even when people around me don't.

Amen

Obeying Equals Love

"Obeying means loving my brother? That doesn't seem fair. Obeying all the rules I have is enough trouble. Now you want me to love my brother, too? Have you met my brother?"

Okay, quit complaining. You don't have to do this by yourself. God will help you. Have you ever actually asked God to help you love someone? Someone you find unlovable? Not that hot guy in your math class.

See, the problem is that God's whole being is based on love. So, if you claim to love God and be His follower, you have to love others.

If there is someone in your world who you're having trouble loving ... better get busy asking God for help!

Dear God.

Help! You know who I'm thinking of. I need lots of Your help to love this person! *Amen*

Anyone who loves God must also love their brother and sister.

1 John 4:21

Protective Gear

CLOTHE
YOURSELVES
WITH THE
LORD
Jesus
Christ.

ROMANS 13:14

It's a cold winter's day. The wind is howling and sharp hard snow pellets are flying through the air, stinging your face and blinding your sight. You've got to walk all the way to school, so you've put on your heavy winter coat, hat, gloves and have a scarf wrapped around your face so nothing shows but little slits of your eyes. You are protected against the weather.

To live a life of obedience to God, you need to put on the right kind of protection against the attacks of Satan. You must clothe yourself with the Lord Jesus Christ. Knowing Him, reading about Him in the Bible, talking to Him every day, trying to model your life after His – that's protection against Satan. Wear Him well!

Dear God,

Thanks for this reminder to protect myself against Satan. Help me to "put on Jesus" every day!

Amen

God's Style

Do you like to wear brightly colored clothes? Maybe you're more of a soft-colored kind of girl. Maybe you only wear blue jeans and a baseball cap. Whatever your choice of clothing, you probably have a certain "look" that you try to maintain. All your clothes have that "look" and lead to your style.

A child of God who lives an obedient life also has a look. She wears compassion, kindness, humility, gentleness and patience and everyone around her will see that. These characteristics may set you apart from other people sometimes. That's good.

Remember every day to put these pieces of clothing on your attitude. It will show that you are God's child.

Dear God,

Some of these things are kind of hard for me. Please fill me with Your love so I can wear these attitudes all the time. *Amen*

"CLOTHE YOURSELVES WITH COMPASSION, kindness, HUMILITY, GENTLENESS & patience.

COLOSSIANS 3:12

Be Humble

Clothe yourself with **HUMILITY** toward one **ANOTHER**, because, "**GOD** opposes the proud but shows favor to the humble."

1 PETER 5:5

People who make themselves super important while they are shoving others down are not obeying God. If a person has to go around spouting how good she is; how smart; how talented; how special ... well then more than likely none of those things are true.

Humble people are God's favored people because humility shows a sensitivity and kindness to others. Humility is others-focused instead of self-focused.

Remember that any talents or abilities you have were given to you by God. You did nothing to gain them so you have nothing to be proud of. Keep your eyes on God first, then focus on others next. Put yourself in last place.

Dear God,

I really want to please You. Help me to obey this command and to be humble. I can't do it by myself. *Amen*

Trust and Obey

Who do you trust? Trust enough to follow someone into a dark forest? Trust enough to let them make choices and decisions for you? It's impossible to obey someone you don't trust. You can't commit your life to obeying someone – even God – if you don't trust that He has your very best interests at heart.

Once you believe that God cares about you and wants you to be happy, successful and have a growing faith, then it's easier to commit your ways to Him. That means seeking His guidance in decisions and with your choice of friends, activities and even your future.

Dear God,

Help me to trust You more and to ask Your guidance in all parts of my life. *Amen*

COMMIT YOUR WAY TO THE LORD; TRUST IN HIM & HE WILL DO THIS: HE WILL MAKE YOUR RIGHTEOUS REWARD SHINE LIKE THE DAWN.

PSALM 37:5-6

Good Communication

DEVOTE YOURSELVES TO PRAYER.

COLOSSIANS 4:2

*D*o you have a best friend? What happens to your friendship if you don't talk to her for a long time? Misunderstandings and hurt feelings kind of creep in, don't they?

It's hard to keep a friendship going well if you don't communicate pretty often. That's one reason God said we should devote ourselves to prayer.

The more we communicate with God, the closer we will be. Remember that praying is not just telling God what you want Him to do or asking Him for stuff. Sometimes prayer means just being still and listening for Him to speak in your heart.

Dear God,

I want to know You better and better. Being still isn't easy, but with Your help I'll be able to do it. I want to hear what You have to say to me.

Amen

All or Nothing

Wholehearted is the key word here. Anything you do with only halfhearted energy is going to fail.

If you put part of your energy into writing a paper for school, it won't be as good as it could be.

If you halfheartedly practice piano, well, it will sound like it. Serving God simply can't be done halfheartedly.

God wants ... demands ... your whole heart 'cause there isn't room in your heart for God and anything else.

Dear God,

I know I'm not wholehearted in serving You. I save room for my friends and stuff I like to do. But, I want to be wholehearted for You. Please help me.   Amen

Acknowledge the GOD of your father, and serve Him with wholehearted devotion and with a willing mind, for the LORD searches every HEART AND understands every DESIRE & every THOUGHT.

1 Chronicles 28:9

Positive Words

ENCOURAGE ONE ANOTHER *daily.*

Hebrews 3:13

Have you ever been to the ocean when the tide is out? The beach is big and wide ... until the waves come back in.

Things in life seem to go in waves sometimes. You can go through a period of time when everything goes wrong, then for no apparent reason things start going right. In the wrong times, nothing you do seems to go the way you planned.

That's when you need encouragement. It helps to know that someone cares about what you're going through. Sometimes you need encouragement and sometimes you need to give encouragement. Pay attention to people around you – obey God by being an encourager.

Dear God,

Help me to notice how my friends and family are feeling. Give me the right words and attitude to be an encourager to them. *Amen*

No Running Away

Watch a small tree some time when the wind is blowing super hard. See how it bends under the pressure of the wind blowing through it? The young tree may bend nearly double in the wind, but it doesn't break and it doesn't blow away. It stands firm – and is made stronger by that exercise of blowing and bending.

Stand firm! Obeying God means standing firm even when you don't see how God can possibly save you or protect you from whatever difficulty you're facing.

This Scripture verse from Exodus is what Moses said to the Israelites just before God parted the waters of the Red Sea to save them. You just never know what God is going to do for you so ... stand firm!

Dear God,

Wow, it takes a lot of faith to stand firm. But, I want to. Help me obey and stand firm. Amen

STAND FIRM and you will see the deliverance the LORD will bring you today.

Exodus 14:13

Listen!

LOVE
THE LORD YOUR
GOD,
LISTEN TO HIS
VOICE,
AND HOLD FAST
TO HIM.

DEUTERONOMY 30:20

The best part of a sandwich cookie is right in the middle! The important part of this verse is right in the middle, too. Be quiet and listen! That's because you know you should love God and you know you should hold on to Him, even if you don't always know how to do that. But, being quiet so you can hear Him — that's tough sometimes.

In this noisy, busy world it isn't easy to make yourself sit down for 15 or 30 minutes and just be quiet — no talking, no music — nothing. But, if you don't get still, how will you ever hear God speak? He won't fight through the noise. He wants you to make the effort.

Choose a Scripture verse, be still and think about it and listen for God to speak.

Dear God,

Please help me with this. I want to learn to be still. I want to listen to You. *Amen*

Walk in Love

When you roll out of bed in the morning do you have to stop and think, "Right foot down; left foot down. Right foot forward. Left foot forward ..."?

Nope, walking comes naturally and you do it without even thinking. Maybe that's the point of this verse – walking in love equals loving without having to think about it.

When you have a difference with another person, settle it immediately – in love.

When you meet someone you don't really like — look for things you can appreciate about her. Walk in love. Everywhere you walk, everywhere you go – be filled with love.

Dear God,

That sounds easy, but it isn't always. I guess that's why You had to make it a command. Please help me walk in love.

Amen

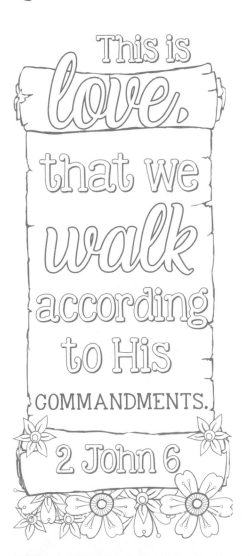

This is love, that we walk according to His COMMANDMENTS.

2 John 6

Active Obedience

BY FAITH ABRAHAM, WHEN **CALLED** TO **GO** TO A PLACE HE WOULD LATER RECEIVE AS **HIS** INHERITANCE, OBEYED AND WENT, EVEN THOUGH HE DID NOT KNOW **WHERE HE** WAS GOING.

HEBREWS 11:8

A gymnast does amazing tricks on the uneven bars, then for her dismount swings high into the air, twists and flips and does a blind landing – she can't see the floor until her feet touch it.

Abraham had a blind landing when God told him to pack up everything and start traveling. He moved his family, servants, animals and belongings ... but God didn't tell Abraham where he was going. Abraham obeyed because he trusted God. He knew that God would direct his path. Whew! That's obedience!

It's hard enough to obey God when you can see where He's leading you. Can you trust Him enough to have a blind landing? You should – remember nothing is unknown to God. He knows exactly where you're going.

Dear God,

Help me to trust You as much as Abraham did. I want to be that obedient!

Amen

Peaceful Words

$\mathcal{A}$ little trickle of water running across a rock seems pretty harmless, doesn't it? Yeah, but if that trickle runs constantly day after day after day ... pretty soon there is a Grand Canyon worn into the rock by that persistent water.

That's the way gossip can break down the unity of God's family. Just a little word here or a comment there and pretty soon the rock is breaking up. God commands us not to let that happen. Make every effort to keep God's family unified and peaceful.

Obeying this command of God means watching every idle comment you are tempted to make – even if it's funny. If it breaks the unity, it's a no-no.

Dear God,

I like making my friends laugh, but I don't want to disobey You. Help me to watch what I say so that no one is hurt by my words. *Amen*

MAKE EVERY effort TO KEEP THE unity OF THE Spirit THROUGH THE bond OF peace.

EPHESIANS 4:3

The Safest Place

"I have heard many reports about this man & all the harm he has done to Your HOLY people..." but the LORD said to Ananias, "GO!"
Acts 9:13, 15

Would God send you into a dangerous situation? If something He asked you to do scared you silly, would He still want you to do it? Yeah. Because He can see a much bigger picture than you can.

In this story from Acts 9, God told Ananias to go talk to Saul. All the Jews knew Saul – he tortured and persecuted them to get them to deny Jesus.

Ananias was more than a little scared. But, God said, "Go," because He knew that Saul had changed and was now a follower of Christ.

The safest place to be is the place where you are obeying God.

Dear God,

I know that some people die while they are obeying You. But, that just means they are with You sooner and that's a good thing! Help me to be brave enough to obey, no matter what You ask.

Amen

Constant Praise

*D*oes it seem kind of funny to be commanded to praise God? Well, sometimes people get so caught up in their problems that they forget how great God is. All they see are the imperfections in their lives and they forget that His works are perfect.

Take your focus off yourself and your problems and think about God. Remember the accounts in the Bible of how He took care of His people and the ways He takes care of you.

Think about His creation – from a tiny flower to mountains, canyons and oceans. God is amazing. Remember to praise Him for His perfect works and just ways!

Dear God,

Thank You for my family, my friends, for horses and puppies. Thank You for mountains and oceans. Thank You for sunrises and sunsets, for rainbows and thunderclouds. Just ... thank You. *Amen*

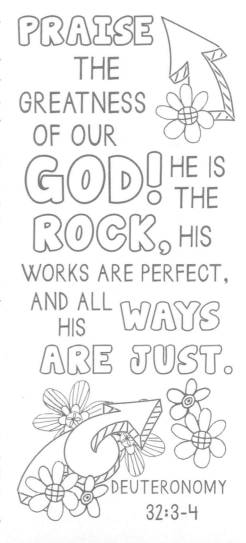

PRAISE THE GREATNESS OF OUR GOD! HE IS THE ROCK, HIS WORKS ARE PERFECT, AND ALL HIS WAYS ARE JUST.

DEUTERONOMY 32:3-4

May

Fighting Temptation

Been There, Done That

Then Jesus was led by the Spirit

INTO THE WILDERNESS TO BE TEMPTED BY THE DEVIL.

MATTHEW 4:1

*D*id you ever shout this at your mom, "You just don't understand"? Most girls do at some point in their lives. Well, that's something you can never say to Jesus. He does understand what it feels like to be tempted because He was!

Now, you understand that Jesus is the Son of God. He didn't have to leave perfect heaven and come down here to live among imperfect people – but He did. Then, He certainly didn't have to experience the powerful temptations that Satan put before Him – but He did ... so He would understand what we go through when we are tempted. So, when temptation is about to yank your heart out, remember to call on Jesus for strength and help. You know He will understand; after all, He's been there.

Dear God,

It helps to know that Jesus really understands how temptation feels. Help me fight off temptation, just as Jesus did! *Amen*

God Will Help You

Slowly stretch a rubber band apart. Pull harder and harder. If you keep pulling, it will eventually break. You will have stretched it beyond its limits.

Maybe you feel like that sometimes – like the temptations of life are too much. Friends may be trying to get you to drink, smoke, or shoplift. Maybe the temptations are more "socially acceptable" like gossip or ripping up someone's reputation. Whatever it is, the constancy of it can stretch you so much that you feel as if you might break. Call on God. He promised that He wouldn't let you be tempted beyond what you can handle.

Ask Him for help and *He will* provide a way out. He promised.

Dear God,

Sometimes I'm tempted to give in 'cause it's just so hard to keep fighting it. Help me, please.

Amen

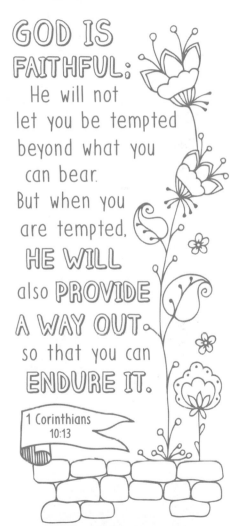

GOD IS FAITHFUL; He will not let you be tempted beyond what you can bear. But when you are tempted, HE WILL also PROVIDE A WAY OUT so that you can ENDURE IT.

1 Corinthians 10:13

Backup!

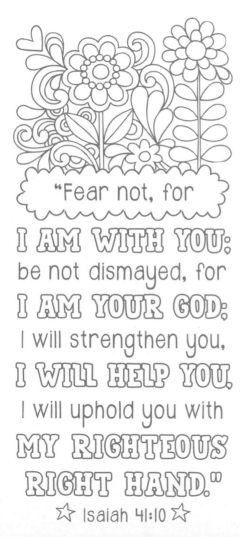

"Fear not, for
I AM WITH YOU;
be not dismayed, for
I AM YOUR GOD;
I will strengthen you,
I WILL HELP YOU,
I will uphold you with
MY RIGHTEOUS
RIGHT HAND."
☆ Isaiah 41:10 ☆

Sometimes on TV cop shows you'll hear one of the policemen call for backup when the bad guys start getting out of hand.

This verse is your backup call. God is ready and willing to help you turn away any temptation that keeps popping up in front of you. Just call on Him.

He promises to strengthen you and help you. Satan is too powerful to fight by yourself. You wouldn't stand a chance on your own.

Call on God to help you fight off whatever Satan throws at you.

Dear God,

I really need Your help. I'm tired of always trying to be strong. Strengthen me with Your power so I can push the temptations away once and for all.

Amen

Dressed for Battle

An athlete doesn't jump into the pro ranks without working her way up through the minor leagues. A singer doesn't sing her first note ever on the Broadway stage. A soldier doesn't go into battle without her weapon and helmet. You must be prepared for what is before you.

Same is true of your spiritual life. There is a battle going on. Satan is trying to knock you down. He's throwing temptation after temptation at you. He's trying to discourage you and chip away at your self-image. The only hope you have of fighting him off is the armor of God – belt of truth, breastplate of righteousness, shield of faith and helmet of salvation. Put your armor on and get in the battle! You can't lose with God on your side.

Dear God,

I've got Your armor on. I can't lose with You on my side!

Amen

THEREFORE TAKE UP THE **WHOLE ARMOR OF GOD,** THAT YOU MAY BE ABLE TO WITHSTAND IN THE EVIL DAY, AND HAVING DONE ALL, TO STAND FIRM.

EPHESIANS 6:13

Are You Strong Enough?

My flesh and my **HEART** may fail, but **GOD** is the **STRENGTH** of my **HEART** and my portion forever. PSALM 73:26

Think you're strong, do ya? Think you can take on the world? Well, here's a news flash ... you aren't as strong as you think. You will stumble and fall sometimes. Humans are not perfect and no matter how hard you try, once in a while you will give in to temptation.

Once in a while you will lose your temper, cheat a little, tell a lie ... something. The good news is that you can turn to God when that happens, confess, ask forgiveness, and start over.

God is your strength forever. He loves you and wants to help you be strong, so keep turning to Him ... even after you've failed. He is always waiting for you to come back.

Dear God,

Thanks for not giving up on me. Thanks for being my strength and for wanting to help me.

Amen

God Is Big

These words from 1 Samuel were spoken by David ... a little kid. He said them to Goliath, a nine-foot-tall experienced soldier. David went to fight Goliath with only a sling and some stones. By all rights he should have been shaking in his sandals.

There was no reason on earth David should have been able to defeat the giant. However, there was a reason in heaven ... God was fighting with David and no giant with a spear and sword had a chance against God.

Whatever you may be facing – trouble with parents, friends, grades, bad choices you've made ... none of it is too big for God to handle. Try Him.

Dear God,

Sometimes I think I've messed my life up so much that it can't be fixed. Thanks for the reminder that nothing is too big for You.

Amen

The BATTLE is the LORD'S.

1 SAMUEL 17:47

God's Investment

This is love, not that we loved God but that He loved us and sent His Son as an atoning sacrifice for our sins. 1 John 4:10

*Y*ou really wanted that cute outfit from that outrageously expensive store. Mom said, "If you want it, save up your money and buy it yourself." So, you did. That outfit represents hours of babysitting runny-nosed kids. So do you throw it on the floor and toss your muddy soccer shoes on top of it?

Hopefully, your investment of time and energy means you take better care of it than that.

God invested in you. He sent His Son, Jesus, to live, die, and be raised back to life ... for you. It makes sense that His investment would mean that He's going to be there when you need His help. He wouldn't invest that much in you, then just turn around and walk away.

Dear God,

I never thought about Your love being like an investment in me. Thanks. I know You will be here to help me, whatever happens. *Amen*

In Your Defense

*D*efense lawyers plead their client's case before a judge and jury. The lawyer points out the defendant's good qualities. He pleads her innocence and requests that she be given another chance.

That's what Jesus does for you. He knows that sometimes you will sin. Therefore, Jesus encourages God to forgive you and give you another chance. Do you see the system God has set up? He loves you so much that not only did Jesus die for you, He now pleads your case before God.

You have to know that means love so, more than anything, God wants to help and strengthen you!

Dear God,

Wow, You must love me so much. I'm so sorry that I don't trust You more. Help me learn to turn to You for help and strength. *Amen*

WE HAVE AN ADVOCATE WITH THE FATHER— JESUS CHRIST, THE RIGHTEOUS ONE.

1 JOHN 2:1

Noisy Airwaves

IN MY DISTRESS
I CALLED TO THE
LORD;
I CRIED TO *my God*
FOR HELP.
FROM HIS TEMPLE
HE HEARD
my voice:
MY CRY CAME
BEFORE
Him, EARS.
INTO HIS

PSALM 18:6

You're at a crowded concert. The auditorium is filled with shouting, screaming fans. Music blares, but the audience is so loud it can barely be heard. You are with a friend who is standing right next to you. Every effort to talk with her is lost in the noise of the crowd. She can't hear a word you say.

Does it sometimes feel like God can't hear your voice? Maybe you think He's too far away or He's busy listening to other people's prayers. Whatever it is, you don't feel like He hears you. The Psalms are filled with reminders that when we call out to God for help, He does hear. He hears and He cares. He will answer.

Dear God,

I want to believe that You hear my prayers and that You will answer them. Please help me believe that more and more. *Amen*

He Knows!

Before you even utter the words, before you even know what you need yourself ... God knows. You see, He can see the big picture, not just what's happening to you right now. He knows what tomorrow will bring and how the circumstances of today will strengthen you for the next thing you have to face. He knows how everything fits together.

He knows when you're going to need extra strength or joy. He knows when you're going to need patience or love. He knows when you need a firm hand or a gentle one. He knows. Trust Him ... and ask Him for His daily help.

Dear God,

That's amazing. You know what I need even before I know! I'm so glad You're in control instead of me! Help me ... every day. *Amen*

"Your Father knows what you need before you ask Him."

Matthew 6:8

The Longest Day

THE SUN STOPPED IN THE MIDDLE OF THE SKY & DELAYED GOING DOWN ABOUT A FULL DAY. THERE HAS NEVER BEEN A DAY LIKE IT BEFORE OR SINCE.  JOSHUA 10:13-14

Joshua and the Israelites were fighting their enemies. Back in those days, when the sun went down the battle was over because the soldiers couldn't see to fight. Joshua knew that if they could just keep fighting, his men would win. So, he asked God to keep the sun from setting so they could keep fighting. God did! The sun and the moon and the stars listened to God – after all, He made them. God kept the sun from setting so Joshua's army could win the battle.

Think about that – it's the same God who is hearing your prayers and fighting for you. Walk close to Him. Obey Him ... and ask Him for what you need!

Dear God,

You really made the sun stand still? That's awesome. You've got more power than anyone ... and You love me! Amazing! *Amen*

Powerful Words

*W*ords are words are words. It's who speaks the words that makes a difference. God spoke the world into existence. The first chapter of Genesis is filled with "And God said ..." while He was busy creating the world and everything in it just by the words He spoke. What amazing power God has.

It is unmatched by anything else in the universe – nothing that is created can be more powerful than the Creator Himself.

There is a little poem that children sometimes learn in Sunday school that goes: "My God is so big, so strong and so mighty. There's nothing my God cannot do!" Keep that in mind when you're thinking that your problems may be too big even for God!

Dear God,

Your words have so much power. There's nothing You can't do. What an awesome God You are!

Amen

Important to Him

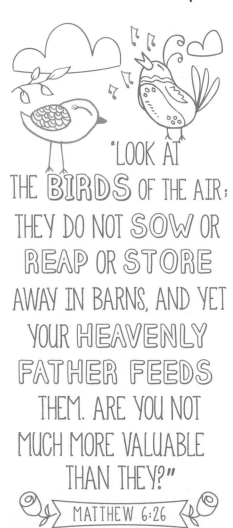

"LOOK AT THE BIRDS OF THE AIR; THEY DO NOT SOW OR REAP OR STORE AWAY IN BARNS, AND YET YOUR HEAVENLY FATHER FEEDS THEM. ARE YOU NOT MUCH MORE VALUABLE THAN THEY?"

MATTHEW 6:26

Do you sometimes feel like a mosquito on an elephant's back ... just a tiny little molecule in the scheme of the whole earth and the millions of people on it? Why should God care about your little problems? After all, they are nothing compared to starving people or children dying of Aids. You're just an average girl with average problems.

Doesn't matter – God loves you. If He takes care of individual birds and makes sure they have food and water, don't you think He's going to take care of you ... His child? He cares about what you care about. Talk to Him. Give Him a chance to help you.

Dear God,

I never thought about You taking care of the birds and all the animals. I guess You want to take care of me, too. Thanks. *Amen*

Black and White

Well, sometimes life is not black and white. Some choices are ... gray. It's hard to know if some things are wrong or right. You know that there isn't any verse that says, "Thou shall not ... whatever," so how do you know if this is a temptation that Satan is dangling in front of you or if is it just a new experience?

Ask God. If you ask Him to show you right from wrong, He will. And He won't make you feel bad for asking. Believe it or not, He wants you to succeed in life. He's not trying to trip you up or trick you into making bad choices. So ... ask Him for wisdom.

Dear God,

Yeah, some decisions aren't easy. Help me know what is right and what is wrong. Thanks.

Amen

If any of you lacks wisdom, you should ask God, who gives generously to all without finding fault, and it will be given to you.

James 1:5

Hang on Tight

Those who wait for the **LORD** shall renew their **STRENGTH;** They shall **mount up** with **WINGS** **LIKE eagles;** they shall run and not **BE WEARY.**

— ISAIAH 40:31

What do you have for breakfast each day? You know the experts say breakfast is the most important meal of the day. That food helps you store up energy to get you through the rest of the day.

Where do you get the spiritual energy to keep on keeping on? By putting your hope and trust in the Lord. He gives the strength and power to make you fly through life and never get spiritually tired again.

Keep leaning on Him. Hang on tight and He'll get you through whatever life brings.

Dear God,

I try to hang on, but my hands get tired. Will You please hang on to me? Thanks. *Amen*

Second Chances

*G*ood old Jonah. God asked him to do a simple job. He refused and hid from God who wasn't fooled at all. Jonah ended up in the belly of a big fish. But he wasn't digested as lunch for the swimming hotel.

He sat there for three days and got to think about his bad choice. Of course, he came to his senses and cried out to God to save him. God did. The fish spat Jonah out and he was able to go about God's business.

You see, wherever you are and whatever you've done, you can still call out to God for help. He can hear you from anywhere and He will forgive your bad choices. So ... what are you waiting for?

Dear God,

Please forgive my bad choices and help me now to make better ones. Give me strength!

Amen

I called out to the Lord, out of my distress, and He ANSWERED me.

Jonah 2:2

Fear Not!

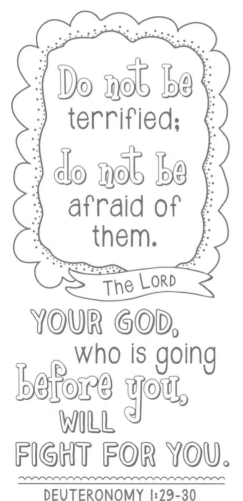

Do not be terrified; do not be afraid of them.

The LORD YOUR GOD, who is going before you, WILL FIGHT FOR YOU.

DEUTERONOMY 1:29-30

Some people never learn. These words are what Moses said to the Israelites when they were too chicken to go into the land God had promised to give them.

They whined that the people were too big and the cities had walls around them. The people forgot about all the miracles God had already done to protect them, including parting the waters of the Red Sea. He fought to save His people.

God will fight for you, too. You are His child and He will take care of you. Whatever problems you're facing or problems you have, remember that you don't have to be afraid. Don't be scared, because God is fighting for you.

Dear God,

Sometimes I am scared. When I get frightened, help me remember that You are fighting for me.

Amen

Priceless

*L*ove is often defined as seeking the highest good for the object (person) of your affections. God loves you – no matter what, He loves you. His love is His motivation to help you become the best person you can be. He will protect you and strengthen you because of that love.

Both powerful important people and small children alike can hide in the shadow of His wings. Just being in His shadow is a place of safety and protection for you.

Any time you're afraid, any time you need help, turn to God. He loves you and He's waiting to show you that.

Dear God,

Every time I think about You loving me it just amazes me. Thank You for showing me Your love by strengthening and helping me through life.

Amen

How priceless is Your unfailing LOVE, O GOD! People take REFUGE in the SHADOW of Your WINGS.

Psalm 36:7

The Battle Rages

YOUR ENEMY
THE DEVIL PROWLS
AROUND LIKE A
roaring
lion
LOOKING FOR
SOMEONE TO DEVOUR.

1 PETER 5:8

You have an enemy. Doesn't matter how nice you are or how pretty. Doesn't matter how kind you are to everyone ... in fact, those things probably make your enemy even more angry. The devil doesn't want you to do anything that even hints at God's love and power. So he's sneaking around like a slime ball looking for ways to trip you up and make you question your own faith.

You can't fight him alone. You just can't. He's too sneaky and tricky. He never gives up. The good news is that you don't have to fight him alone. God is there to help you. Ask Him for strength and wisdom to fight your enemy. God wants you to win. He will help.

Dear God,

It's kind of scary to think that the devil is out to get me. I need Your strength every day to resist him. Help me, please. *Amen*

Never Alone

What a comfort. You're not in the battle alone. Never. God hasn't walked away to deal with someone else. He's with you always.

There isn't anyone more important to Him than you. He knows the temptations you face every day. He knows when the devil is trying to knock you down. He knows when you're sad and discouraged and He is right there with you. Even in times when you can't "feel" God with you, He's there.

So, what does that mean for you? It means you can ask for God's help and strength and He will answer. He's right beside you and in those times when you are too upset or discouraged to even pray – He knows what you need.

Dear God,

Thanks for never leaving me. Thanks for helping me every day to live for You. *Amen*

"NEVER WILL I LEAVE YOU; NEVER WILL I FORSAKE YOU."

HEBREWS 13:5

Close to God

"If you remain **IN ME** and My words remain **IN YOU,** ask whatever you wish, and it will be done for you."
— John 15:7

*W*hat do you want to ask God? Is there something that you have been too scared to ask Him? Did it seem like a silly request or maybe too gutsy? Lay the right foundation here – remain in Him.

That means stay close to Him. Spend time with Him every day and talk with Him. When you do that, you begin to think more like Him. You begin to want what He wants which means your requests are things He knows are right for you. Then you can ask Him whatever is on your mind and He will answer.

Dear God,

Most of the time I'm asking You for stuff. I'd like to get to the point where I'm thinking like You. Then when I pray, I know I'm praying in the direction You want me to. *Amen*

Nothing Is Too Hard

Of course, your immediate answer to that question is: "No – nothing is too hard for the Lord." After all, you know that God created everything. You've read the stories of how He parted the Red Sea and made the sun stand still. You've heard how He knocked down the walls of Jericho. You know all about that stuff.

So ... if you know how strong and powerful He is, why don't you trust Him to help you with your life?

If God can part the Red Sea, He can deal with bully classmates. If God can make the sun stand still, He can handle the temptations you have. Nothing is too hard for Him, including the stuff in your life.

Dear God,

I guess I never realized that I've been holding out asking for Your help 'cause maybe I thought the stuff in my life was too hard for You. I'm sorry. Please forgive me. *Amen*

Is anything too HARD for the LORD?

Genesis 18:14

Growing and Learning

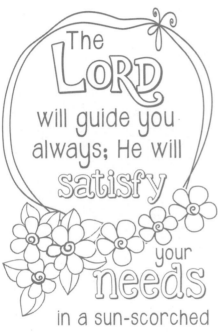

The **LORD** will guide you always; He will **satisfy** your **needs** in a sun-scorched land and will strengthen **your frame.** You will be like a **well-watered garden.**

—ISAIAH 58:11

Life is a learning process. Babies can't talk or walk when they are first born. Children need help learning how to read and write. They also need to grow some before they can make good decisions such as when it's safe to cross a street.

Until children grow up, their parents must help them with decisions and guide them.

The same is true of spiritual growth. God guides His children, helping them learn to make good choices and to resist the tricks of the devil.

God will take care of you and help you grow.

Dear God,

I want to grow and learn. Thank You for being my guide and teacher along the way. *Amen*

Big Love

*H*ave you ever been to the mountains or to the ocean? Were you overwhelmed by how large and massive they are? God's love for you is bigger. Ask God to help you understand how much He loves you.

Once you begin to understand that, you will believe that He will help you with anything you need. That much love brings so much strength, power, hope and help.

God will step in and help you fight temptation. He will help you grow and learn because He loves you.

Dear God,

I think Your love is bigger than anything I can imagine. Please help me see how much You love me. That will help me trust You more. *Amen*

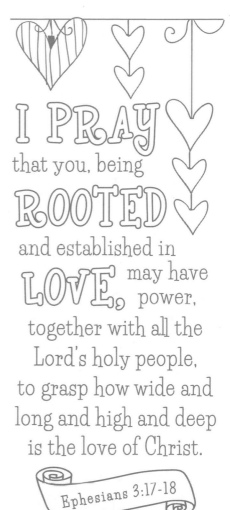

I PRAY that you, being ROOTED and established in LOVE, may have power, together with all the Lord's holy people, to grasp how wide and long and high and deep is the love of Christ.

Ephesians 3:17-18

Staying on Track

WHEN MY SPIRIT GROWS FAINT WITHIN ME, IT IS YOU WHO WATCH OVER MY WAY

PSALM 142:3

*B*eing tired and discouraged can make you want to give up on things. If you've been fighting temptations for a long time, or if you have felt like everything you do goes wrong, you may feel like giving up. What's the use of fighting it? Just go with the crowd and do the things they do. Maybe that's what you were meant to do.

These times of discouragement are when you need to turn to God. He knows that your strength is weak. He will help you stay on the right path – the path of obedience to Him. He knows the way you should go and if you ask Him, He will keep you on that path.

Dear God,

Please help me stay on the path that You want me to be on. Guide and direct me. *Amen*

A Hiding Place

Do you have a special place where you go to be alone? Some people have a special spot in the house, some climb up in a tree and hide among the branches and leaves, some have a quiet place in a garden or park. These are places where you can be alone to think and be quiet. They are refuges – places hidden away from the noisy, busy world.

God is a refuge. He is the place to go when life gets too hard. When your parents are screaming at each other again. When your mom is on your case for the thirtieth time today, when school is too hard, when your friends are being jerks. God is a refuge because He cares what you're going through.

Dear God,

I need a refuge. Thanks for being there.

Amen

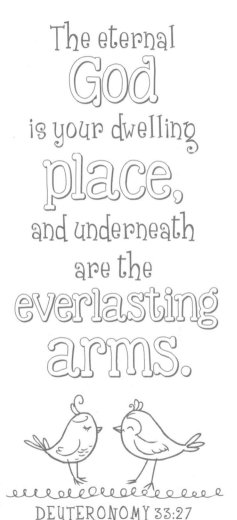

The eternal God is your dwelling place, and underneath are the everlasting arms.

DEUTERONOMY 33:27

Stay Close

Draw NEAR TO GOD & He will draw NEAR TO you.

James 4:8

*W*hat happens if you accidentally lock yourself out of the house? Do you call your dad who is on a business trip half way around the country?

He will care about your problem, but he can't help. Do you call your mom who is working twenty-five miles away? She'll help, but not immediately. Do you call the next-door neighbor who has a spare key to your house? Bingo – the person who is closest to you is the best one to call.

Think about that in relation to God. God never moves away from you – you move away from Him. The time to come close to Him is not when there are major problems in your life. Get close now ... and stay there. Then, when you need His help, He's right there!

Dear God,

The best place to be is close to You, my strength and help. I want to spend time with You every day so that I'm really close.

Amen

Perfect Power

Were you ever given a really cool present for no reason at all? It wasn't your birthday or Christmas. Did that make you feel special? When you opened it, you probably realized that the person who gave it to you must care about you a lot.

That's the way God's grace is – you didn't do anything to earn it. He just gives it because He loves you. He wants to help you with decisions and problems by sharing His power with you. That doesn't mean that He has to come down to your human level.

By sharing His power with you, His power grows. That's how God's love is – sharing it makes it grow. Cool, huh?

Dear God,

Thank You for helping me in my weakness. You are so strong!

Amen

"My grace is sufficient for you, for My power is made perfect in weakness."

2 Corinthians 12:9

Shaped by the Potter

"LIKE CLAY IN THE HAND OF THE *potter,* SO *are you* IN MY *hand.*

JEREMIAH 18:6

*A*potter begins his work by putting a big glob of wet clay on his potter's wheel. He works with it, shaping it gently but firmly, tossing water on it when it gets too dry. The potter patiently shapes the clay into the piece of pottery that he knew it could be. The result is a beautiful, useful piece of pottery.

God says that you are like that piece of clay in His hand. He will shape you and form you into the person He knows you can be. That means when you have problems and need His help, He will be there. He will use problems and stresses as well as happiness and joy to shape your life.

Dear God,

Sometimes it hurts to be shaped like pottery. Help me remember that You are helping me become a better person by the things in my life.

Amen

Power Source

You might be surprised to know that God never promised you happiness. What He did promise is that if you will stay close to Him, He will help you find purpose in your life. He will show you what your gifts are and how He wants to use them.

He promised over and over that He will help you with the tough times in life, if you will turn to Him. When you've got problems, don't put your hope in stuff or in people. Decide right now that you will automatically turn to God and trust His power. Then stay close to Him on a daily basis so you won't have far to turn!

Dear God,

I know I need to read Your Word and talk to You every day so that I'm connected to You — my Power Source. *Amen*

BE STRONG IN THE LORD AND IN THE STRENGTH OF HIS MIGHT

EPHESIANS 6:10

Believe in His Love

The check-out line in the grocery store is a classic place to see a two-year-old throw a temper tantrum. The little cutie sees the candy rack and starts grabbing. Mom gently says, "No," and puts the candy back.

The child registers her desires by screaming, kicking, and throwing herself down on the floor. Submitting to mom's decision is not an easy or popular choice. But you didn't ever do that, did you?

Submitting is not easy if you don't give up your own will. If you're going to resist obeying God and His guidance in your life, you will have problems. The key here is to understand that God loves you. Submitting to Him will bring good things for you.

Dear God,

I guess trusting You has to come before submitting to You. You can't help me with stuff until I do both of those things. Please help me trust You more.

Amen

JAMES 4:7

Not an Option

"GO and make disciples of all nations, baptizing them in the name of the Father and of the Son and of the Holy Spirit, and teaching them to obey EVERYTHING I have commanded you."

MATTHEW 28:19-20

Sharing the message of God's love is not an option. You can't shrug your shoulders and say, "That's for grown-ups to do." It doesn't say, "Everyone over twenty-five should go and make disciples ..." Nope, the truth is that kids might listen to someone their own age better than they would an adult. This doesn't mean you have to stand behind a pulpit and preach a sermon. You can start being a witness by just living your life for God.

There's a saying that your life may be the only Bible some people will ever read. Don't be afraid to make choices that reflect your love for God and obedience to Him.

Dear God,

Help me live so that others can see my love for You.

Amen

Sharing the Gospel

Witnessing is like ripples. You know, when you toss a pebble into a puddle of water, the ripples start small around where the pebble went into the water. Then they get larger as they spread out from that spot. Jesus said you should start witnessing right where you are – with your close friends and family. That's your Jerusalem.

Then the ripples spread to your Judea – your school, and your larger group of friends. Then you may get a chance to go to Samaria and the ends of the earth on short-term mission trips or things like that. You never know what God has planned for you. For right now ... just take care of your Jerusalem.

Dear God,

Witnessing kind of scares me. Help me live in a way that shows how much I love You. Give me the right words when I get a chance to share. Thanks.

Amen

"YOU will receive power when the HOLY SPIRIT has come upon you, and you WILL BE MY WITNESSES."

Acts 1:8

Stop, Look and Worship

> Then those who were in the boat **worshiped Him,** saying, "Truly You are the **Son of GOD."**
>
> MATTHEW 14:33

What is a witness? Simply stated, a witness is someone who has seen something. The disciples saw Jesus do all kinds of miracles. This verse describes their response to seeing Him walking on the water to their boat. They worshiped Him. "Well, duh," you say, "if God did some super-miracle for me, I'd worship Him, too." Well, duh, yourself.

Look around you. God does miracles for you every day – the sun comes up, the stars stay in their places, the oceans don't overrun the earth, you have a family who loves you, He helps you make choices that keep you in one piece. You've gotten so used to miracles that you expect them to happen day after day. Stop, look and worship Him for them.

Dear God,

I guess I do have stuff to witness about. Help me remember to share it with others. *Amen*

Fear Not!

*O*ral book reviews ... words that strike fear in the hearts of students! Public speaking is one of the biggest fears many people have. I guess it makes sense that witnessing would be included in that.

There is the fear of sharing your faith in public, fear of them rejecting what you say – or worse – making fun of you, and the fear of not getting it right. Whew! Lots to be afraid of.

Take courage and start with what you know. Obey the Ten Commandments and that obedience and love for others will set you apart from the world. Your life will become a witness before you ever have to speak a word.

Dear God,

Help me remember that my friends will notice how I live and what I say. Help me to be a witness for You.

Amen

"Be strong AND VERY courageous. BE CAREFUL TO OBEY ALL THE LAW MY SERVANT MOSES GAVE YOU; DO NOT TURN FROM IT TO THE right OR TO THE left, THAT YOU MAY BE successful WHEREVER YOU GO."

JOSHUA 1:7

Excitement!

The disciples were overjoyed when they saw the Lord.

JOHN 20:20

Christmas morning. Presents are piled around the tree – big ones and small ones. One package could be ... might be ... the one thing you want so much you can taste it.

The family slowly makes its way through the gift-opening process and finally, that one box is in front of you – wonder of wonders! It is exactly what you wanted. *You are overjoyed!* You can't wait to tell your friends!

When you know something that is great news or when you get something that is awesome, you want to tell people! That's where witnessing comes in. When the disciples understood who Jesus was, they wanted to tell people. What's your response when you get excited about God's love for you?

Dear God,

I want to be excited about You. I want to be so excited that I just tell everyone! *Amen*

Harvest Time!

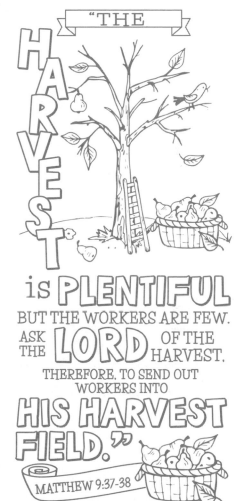

"THE **HARVEST** is PLENTIFUL BUT THE WORKERS ARE FEW. ASK THE **LORD** OF THE HARVEST, THEREFORE, TO SEND OUT WORKERS INTO **HIS HARVEST FIELD.**"

MATTHEW 9:37-38

*W*hat would happen if a farmer had fields of grain ready to be harvested, but no workers to pick the grain? Everything in the fields would all rot and go to waste.

God's harvest is the people of the world – the people who need to know Him in order to be saved. There are literally hundreds of thousands of people who might choose to accept Jesus, but ... no one has told them about Him. The workers are few – some people aren't doing their job of being Christ's witnesses.

It's not a job for just certain people; it's a job for everyone who believes in Jesus. How are you doing at this job?

Dear God,

It's kinda scary to tell people about You. Please help me. Give me the right words to say and the courage to say them. *Amen*

Do Your Job

I PLANTED THE SEED, APOLLOS WATERED IT, BUT GOD HAS BEEN MAKING IT grow.

I CORINTHIANS 3:6

"Witness? You want me to tell someone about God? You want me to help someone be saved? I can't do that. I'm just a kid. Are you crazy? It's too much!" Alright ... calm down, kid. You don't have to do it all by yourself. Witnessing and helping people get saved is a team effort.

Maybe you plant the seed by just living your life for Christ. Maybe someone else waters it by sharing Bible verses with the same person. But, only God can bring a person to Himself.

Sometimes you might be the seed planter. Sometimes you might be the water girl. The point is ... you are willing to do what God wants you to do.

Dear God,

When I see that witnessing is a team thing, that makes it easier. Help me to just take the opportunities You give me. *Amen*

Best Kept Secret

Praising God cannot be a private thing. If you just worship and praise Him in the privacy of your room or even in the safety of your church, well you are missing something.

The truth is that if you're embarrassed or scared of what your friends might think about your relationship with God, then you probably don't feel free to really worship Him.

If you can't praise Him and thank Him with all your heart, then it's going to be pretty hard to tell others about Him. So, where are you on this? Is God the best kept secret you ever had?

Dear God,

Okay, I admit that sometimes I'm nervous about what my friends think about me being a Christian. Help me to get over it and let my love for You grow.   *Amen*

PRAISE the LORD. Give THANKS to the LORD, for He is GOOD. HIS LOVE ENDURES FOREVER.

Psalm 106:1

Time Is Running Out

"As long as it is *day*, we must do the *works* of Him who sent Me. *Night* is *coming*, when no one can *work*."

John 9:4

When you have a big project to do for school, do you wait until the last minute to start it? Then you stay up all night writing the paper and gathering your visuals, checking your references and hoping that you get it finished. If you've waited too late to start, well, you run out of time.

That's the point Jesus was making in this verse. Some people look around at their family and friends and think, "Yeah, they need to hear about God, but there will be time to tell them later." Jesus' reminder is that eventually time runs out and it will be too late to witness. Do the work while there's still time!

Dear God,

I guess I've thought that there will always be another chance to tell my friends about You. I know now that time is going to run out eventually. Help me to get busy! *Amen*

Salt of the Earth

You're different ... well, you're supposed to be. As much as you try to dress like everyone else, have the same brand of shoes, same kind of backpack, like the same music ... all those things ... you're supposed to be different. What does salt do for food? Gives it flavor. It prevents it from spoiling.

Jesus said that you ... one of His children ... can do those same things. You should be different in the way you treat others, even your parents, how you respect authority, how you handle problems. You should give a God-like flavor to your world. That's witnessing with your life.

Dear God,

To be salt I need to be thinking about You all the time — even when it's hard and I'm hanging out with my friends. Help me to be salt to them.

Amen

"You are THE salt of the earth. BUT IF THE SALT LOSES ITS saltiness, HOW CAN IT BE MADE salty AGAIN? IT IS NO LONGER GOOD FOR anything." MATTHEW 5:13

Light Up the World!

"YOU ARE THE LIGHT OF THE WORLD. A TOWN BUILT ON A HILL CANNOT BE HIDDEN."

MATTHEW 5:14

A light shining in darkness can be seen from a great distance, even a small light! It lights up everything around it – things can be seen that would be lost in the darkness. Jesus said that a Christian (that's you, kiddo) is a light in a world full of people who are literally dying.

People will eventually come toward the light because the darkness gets pretty discouraging. Witnessing doesn't have to be a big scary thing. It's just living – living in obedience to God. It means you can't act one way with your friends and another way at church. It's important that you live for God all the time. Be a light.

Dear God,

It's so hard to live for You in front of my friends sometimes. Help me, please. Give me courage.

Amen

Living Real

*F*akin' it – ever tried it? You know, pretending that you like someone when you really don't. Faking that you've studied for a test when you haven't. Or faking that you pray every day and really care about what God wants for you.

You can fool people. You can even fake witnessing about who God is. But, you can't fool God. He looks at the heart and knows what your motives truly are.

The Pharisees were fakers. They acted religious, but in their hearts they didn't care at all about God. If you're just faking your relationship with God, don't bother. No, just stop it and get real. Live for God and let your life be a witness for Him.

Dear God,

I don't want to be a faker. Help me be real.

Amen

"FOR I TELL YOU THAT UNLESS YOUR RIGHTEOUSNESS SURPASSES THAT OF THE PHARISEES AND THE TEACHERS OF THE LAW, CERTAINLY NOT ENTER THE KINGDOM OF HEAVEN."

MATTHEW 5:20

In Training

For the *eyes of the* LORD range throughout the earth to *strengthen* those whose *hearts* are fully committed to Him.
— 2 Chronicles 16:9 —

*G*etting prepared. That's key. A weight lifter doesn't start his career by lifting 500 pounds. A marathoner doesn't run 26 miles the first time she puts on her running shoes. An athlete of any kind begins her career by training. She builds up her muscles and her lung strength in preparation to be able to do her best.

Aren't you glad to hear that the same thing is true in the Christian life? You are in training! You start by giving your heart to God and He keeps strengthening you to do His work. He's always watching out for you, too. He's watching to see when you need His help.

Dear God,

Thank You for strengthening me. Thank You for helping me. *Amen*

Live with Purpose

*W*hat does it mean to give an account? Well, every month the bank sends a report of what is in your bank account. That is an account. On the other hand, giving an account of your life to God means that you explain what you have been doing with your life. How are you spending your time and energy? God's going to ask you.

You see, God has given people a basic job to do – obey Him and live for Him and share the news with people around you. The day will come when God will ask you to give an account of your life. Begin right now to live your life with purpose so your account will be good.

Dear God,

I want to live on purpose so my account to You will be good. Please help me.   *Amen*

SO THEN, EACH OF US WILL GIVE AN ACCOUNT OF OURSELVES TO GOD.

ROMANS 14:12

Witness to Love

THEY TELL OF THE **GLORY OF** YOUR *kingdom* AND SPEAK OF YOUR **MIGHT,** SO THAT ALL PEOPLE MAY KNOW OF YOUR *mighty* **ACTS** AND THE GLORIOUS SPLENDOR OF YOUR *kingdom.*

PSALM 145:11-12

So ... do you think, "I can't witness about God. I wouldn't know what to talk about." These two verses are a clue. When you witness you talk about the glory of His kingdom and His might. Don't you think your friends and family would be happy to learn about God's kingdom – a perfect place filled with love? It's also a comfort to think about His mighty acts because they show His almighty power.

Maybe you don't feel like you see His power in your own everyday life, but you do see it in nature and you know the stories in the Bible. You can witness about those. Most of all, you should witness about His constant, wonderful love.

Dear God,

I know You love me. Help me to tell others that You love them, too.

Amen

Never Too Young

Jeremiah was one of the greatest prophets who ever served God. But, when God first called him to serve, Jeremiah said, "I can't serve You, I'm too young!" He wasn't, of course, because anyone, no matter how young they are, can serve God.

God has called you, too, to do something for Him. It may not be to preach or teach ... it might be to just be friends with someone who needs to know that God loves her.

Whatever He wants you to do, if you stay close to Him by reading His Word and praying, He will give you the words to speak when the time is right.

Dear God,

Wow, even Jeremiah thought he was too young. I guess if You helped him, You will help me, too.

Amen

The LORD said to me, "Do not say, 'I am too young.' You must go to everyone I send you to and say whatever I command you ... I have put My words in your mouth."

Jeremiah 1:7, 9

Growing Up!

PROVERBS 12:15

THE WAY OF FOOLS SEEMS right TO THEM, BUT THE wise listen to advice.

The *terrible twos!* Parents hear stories about how stubborn their darling children are going to become when they hit two years old ... and it's usually true. But then as the child gets older she gets a bit wiser and begins to want to learn and listen to advice.

Sometimes it's scary to think about telling your friends about the Lord because you think they wouldn't care anyway. Be careful about that. Sometimes they want to learn. They want advice on how to live in this world. They just might be waiting to hear what you have to say!

Dear God,

I never thought of that. Maybe my friends are just waiting for me to tell them about You. Give me the right time and the right words to tell them!

Amen

The Most Important Topic

You can probably talk with your friends about anything – problems with your parents – how they do not understand you – that their rules are old-fashioned; that you have way too many chores to do; teachers – good ones and bad ones – who give too much homework; people at school – cool ones and totally weird ones; clothes, music ... well, on and on.

But the one topic that is hardest to bring up is definitely the most important – God. It's scary because you don't want your friends to feel like you think you're better than them. You don't want them to think you're the weird one! What do you do about this fear? Pray ... ask God to help you. Then, remember that He will help and there is nothing to be afraid of!

Dear God,

Okay. Help me talk with my friends about You. Give me the courage to speak up. *Amen*

The Lord is my helper; I will not be afraid.

Hebrews 13:6

The Real You

Jesus said to them, "A PROPHET is not without HONOR except in his OWN TOWN and in his OWN HOME."

Matthew 13:57

One place where it's very hard to talk about Jesus is ... at home. After all, your parents and brothers and sisters know the *real you*. They know your temper fits, when you tell a little lie or don't do your chores. They see your bad attitudes and the times you aren't loving. It's hard to talk about God and live for Him when these people see the times you don't.

That's okay, Jesus knew it would be hard. He knew that the people you love the most would be the hardest to talk to about Him. Ask Him to help you live in a loving and obedient way so your family will notice.

Dear God,

Sometimes my family makes me so mad. But I do really love them and I want them to know You. Help me live for You in front of them – all the time.

Amen

God Knows

*P*hilip was just minding his own business, when God told him to talk to this guy. Philip was confused because the guy was a government official – kinda scary to talk about God to someone who is so important.

But, what do ya know? The guy was actually reading the Bible but he didn't understand it. So, Philip explained it to him and the guy got it!

When you feel that nudge to talk to someone about God – don't fight it. God knows the whole picture of what that person is going through and what they are thinking about. He knows when the time is right. Don't question Him, just obey!

Dear God,

Help me listen and obey. Help me remember that You know the whole story.

Amen

"Do you understand what you are **READING?**" Philip asked.

"HOW CAN I," he said, "unless someone **EXPLAINS IT TO ME?"**

Acts 8:30-31

Proving Your Work

Always be **PREPARED** to give an **ANSWER** to **EVERYONE** who asks you to **GIVE THE REASON FOR THE HOPE** that you have.
— 1 Peter 3:15

*A*re you able to come up with the right answer to a complicated math problem? Then the teacher asks you to prove your work – show how you arrived at the answer. Sometimes that's the hard part.

Maybe you're pretty good at living the Christian life. For the most part you are able to control gossiping and bad attitudes. Maybe you're pretty good at letting your friends see that you trust God. But, at some point one of them may ask you why your life is different.

You need to have answers ready to give them. Pray about that right now and ask the Lord to help you be ready to give that answer.

Dear God,

I thought that if I just live right that's enough and I'll never have to actually say anything ... so, would You help me be ready with the right words? Thanks.

Amen

Ambassadors

What does an ambassador do? An ambassador from one country goes to another country to spread good feelings about his homeland. He is a representative. You have the opportunity to be Christ's ambassador – spread good feelings and good news about Him.

Actually, whether you admit it or not you are an ambassador for something. Either you stand for Christ or you stand against Him. There really isn't a middle of the road here.

Not making a choice to serve Him is to actually make a choice NOT to serve Him. Take on the responsibility and recognize that you are His ambassador – live strong for Him!

Dear God,

I want to be the best ambassador You've ever had. Help me live strong for You!

Amen

WE ARE THEREFORE Christ's AMBASSADORS, as though God were making HIS APPEAL through US.

2 Corinthians 5:20

Tell Others

Leaving her **water jar**, the **woman** went back to the town and said to the people, "Come, see a **man** who told me **everything I ever did**. Could this be the **Messiah?**"

John 4:28-29

Stubborn love. That's what Jesus had for this woman. She had a messy life. She had been married several times and was living with some dude she wasn't married to. She had made bad choices. Plus, she had a rotten attitude. Here she was talking to Jesus Himself ... and she was pretty snippy! Jesus didn't walk away though.

He kept talking, kept loving and finally the walls around her heart broke open. Then, what did she do? She ran to tell others about Him, becoming an instant witness. That's what excitement and joy does. That's what understanding does. Do you understand how much He loves you?

Do you understand how much He loves everyone? Then ... tell them!

Dear God,

I want to be as excited as this woman was. Fill me with joy and excitement so I can tell others, too.

Amen

One Way!

A one-way sign beside the road means ... you can only go in one direction on that street. If you try to go the other way, you'll get a ticket and probably cause an accident.

There are lots of "ways to get to heaven" being thrown around in our world today. Maybe some of your friends have embraced some of those ideas. The sad thing is that they aren't true. The way to heaven is through accepting Jesus as your Savior.

One way – no other doors and no other paths. You've got the truth! Cool, huh? But you also must find a way to share that truth with your friends. Don't let them believe a lie.

Dear God,

Give me the words to speak and the right time to speak them. I want my friends to know You.

Amen

There is no other name under heaven given among MEN by which we must be saved.

Acts 4:12

Anyone Can Be Saved

ALL THOSE WHO HEARD HIM WERE **astonished** AND ASKED, "ISN'T HE THE MAN **who raised** HAVOC IN JERUSALEM AMONG THOSE WHO **call on** THIS [CHRIST'S] **name?"**

ACTS 9:21

Saul was a nasty guy. He made it his life's work to find people who believed in Christ and make their lives *miserable*. He was good at it, too.

If there ever was a person you would think couldn't be saved, it would be Saul. But, lo and behold, Jesus got hold of Saul's heart and it was changed. Saul became Paul – one of the greatest preachers of all time and the guy God used to write lots of chapters in His Word, the Bible.

Do you know someone who is so bad that you think she could never be saved? Someone so mean that you think she would never want to know about God? Don't be so sure. Changing the heart is God's work, not yours.

Dear God,

I'll leave the heart-changing to You. I'll just do what You want me to do and not worry if the people I talk to decide to follow You. *Amen*

The Beginning

ALL HAVE SINNED AND FALL SHORT OF THE GLORY OF GOD.

ROMANS 3:23

*B*asic information here. Everyone who ever lived on this earth is a sinner. That began with Adam and Eve. Everyone needs to know that Jesus came to earth, lived and taught, was crucified, died and rose again. He did all this for one reason – love.

The fact is that the good things people do won't get them into heaven. The good things they do don't mean they aren't sinners anymore. Everyone probably knows deep in their own hearts that they have bad thoughts and selfish motives. What people need to realize is that God knows that, too.

This is basic information that a person must understand before she believes she needs God in her life.

Dear God,

I can always explain away my sin and I guess others do, too. Help me understand this basic information in my life and be able to explain it to others. We are sinners ... all of us. *Amen*

The Price Is Paid

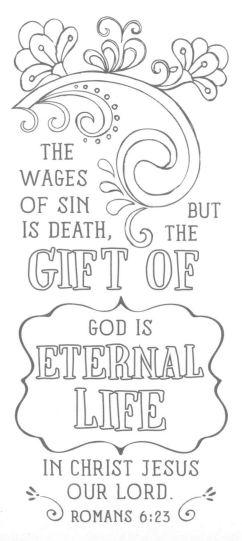

THE WAGES OF SIN IS DEATH, BUT THE GIFT OF GOD IS ETERNAL LIFE IN CHRIST JESUS OUR LORD.
ROMANS 6:23

You get what you pay for." You may buy a shirt that looks exactly like a designer brand. It isn't though, it's a knock-off brand that is a lot cheaper. But, after a while you may discover that it doesn't hold up as well as the real thing. The seams come loose or it loses its shape or the color fades – well, you got what you paid for.

The same is true of sin. If a person chooses to live a sinful life, ignoring God, there is a price to pay – eternal death. No heaven.

The good news you can share with others is that God took care of that. He paid the price for you! Jesus' death and resurrection opened the door to heaven and eternal life! Good news to tell everyone, right?

Dear God,

Thank You for opening that door. It's good news that I want to tell others. Amen

No Grudges

*I*f you have a sister or brother, you know that sometimes life gets nasty at home. Your little brother can be a real creep and make you so stinking mad that you just want to lock him in the bathroom for about five years! So, when you're really angry at someone who has been mean to you, are you ever tempted to do something nice for him ... for no reason? Probably not.

But think about this. People are sinners ... all people. Even knowing that people were going to continually disobey Him and disappoint Him, God showed His incredible love by sending His Son, Jesus, to die for our sins. That's news worth sharing.

Dear God,

Wow, that's amazing. I need to tell others how much You love them.

Amen

GOD SHOWS HIS Love FOR US IN THAT WHILE WE WERE STILL SINNERS, Christ DIED FOR US. ROMANS 5:8

Serious Stuff

ANYONE WHOSE **NAME** WAS NOT FOUND **WRITTEN** IN THE **BOOK OF LIFE** WAS THROWN INTO **THE LAKE** OF FIRE.

REVELATION 20:15

God does not deal in empty threats. Some people make empty threats like, "Clean your room or you're grounded ... get your grades up or you'll be yanked out of school." Empty threats – some could be carried out and some couldn't. But, pretty soon you don't believe any of the threats that person makes.

Well, hear this – when God says that a person has to accept Jesus to come to heaven, that's no empty threat. Hell is a real place and if God's children don't witness to people so they know about God's love, well, their names will not be in the Book of Life ... and they won't be able to come into heaven. Serious stuff.

Dear God,

Sometimes it's hard to believe that hell is a real place. I don't want any of the people I love to go there. Help me tell them about You. *Amen*

Domino Effect

Have you ever set dominos? When you tip the first one it falls and knocks down all the ones behind it. That's what is called the domino effect.

God never intended for it to be hard for people to know how to get to heaven. He gave us a whole Book of instructions. He told His children to spread the news. God would be thrilled if every single person who ever lived had their names written in the Book of Life. Each person has to choose to follow God, but they can't choose until they know about Him.

That's where God's children come in – witnessing – telling others about God's love. Somebody told you the Good News, shouldn't you tell someone else, then they should tell someone, too? Pass on the Good News!

Dear God,

I understand my responsibility. Help me know what to say and when to say it. Amen

You make known to me the path of life; in your presence THERE IS FULLNESS of joy. Psalm 16:11

July

The Best Me
I Can Be

Get Off the Fence

There is an old saying that goes, "Stand for something or you'll fall for anything." Step number one in becoming the best you that you can be is to decide what foundation you're going to stand on. Will you choose to obey God and honor Him even if family and friends around you do not?

If you've been riding the fence – acting one way when you hang out with certain friends and another way when you're with your church friends – well, that won't cut it.

Make a choice to obey God. That's the foundation to build the rest of your life on!

Dear Lord,

Okay, so I have to make a choice. Trying to keep a foot in both worlds is a lot of work anyway. I choose You.

Amen

Blessed are those who fear the Lord, who find great delight in His commands.

Psalm 112:1

Watch Your Mouth

Words can get you into so much trouble! From losing your temper and spouting off to gossip to just plain old unkind words. How many times have your feelings been hurt by what someone else has said? You know how hard it is to forget those unkind words. They lie on your heart like a steel blanket that you just can't get rid of.

Your unkind words do the same thing to others. You don't want to be the reason someone is sad, discouraged or depressed, do you? Watch what you say. It's possible to speak in love, even when you are disagreeing with someone. You don't have to attack another person to disagree with her. Remember that you are God's representative, so watch your mouth.

Dear Lord,

Sometimes words just seem to roll out of my mouth. Help me to guard my mouth. *Amen*

THOSE WHO GUARD THEIR LIPS PRESERVE THEIR LIVES, BUT THOSE WHO SPEAK RASHLY WILL COME TO RUIN.

PROVERBS 13:3

Make a Change

DO NOT

CONFORM

TO THE PATTERN
OF THIS

WORLD,

BUT BE TRANSFORMED
BY THE RENEWING
OF YOUR MIND.

~ ROMANS 12:2 ~

If you keep doing things the same old way, you're going to get the same old results. If you watch TV all day while eating chips and candy – you'll never lose weight and get physically fit. If you don't do your homework – you'll keep failing classes. You get the idea.

Becoming the best you possible may involve getting away from the habits and activities of your "old" life. Renew your mind by reading God's Word and talking with Him. Stop doing the things that you know are disobedient to Him.

You gotta make a choice to make a change.

Dear Lord,

I want to change because I want to make a difference for You.

Amen

A Healthy Heart

"THE mouth SPEAKS WHAT THE heart IS FULL OF."

Luke 6:45

You are so hungry and thirsty that you think you just might faint. You grab some cookies and pour a glass of cold milk. You gobble up a cookie and take a big gulp of milk and ... *yuck!* The milk is sour. That stinks – it didn't look any different from fresh milk.

Yeah, things can look good on the outside, but when their insides are examined the truth comes out. If your heart is full of bad stuff like selfishness and anger, it's going to show on the outside, usually through the words you speak or the way you act.

Take care of your heart.

Dear Lord,

I know that some of the stuff in my heart is bad. Help me get rid of that stuff and fill my heart with love. *Amen*

What Really Matters

If I give all I possess to the poor and give over my body to hardship that I may **boast,** but do not have **love,** I gain nothing.

1 Corinthians 13:3

*A*fter a big disaster people around the world become very generous. They volunteer their services. Others send money. Still others send food and clothing. Maybe you've done some of these things, too. Good for you, we should always help our neighbors.

But, here's a question: How do you treat your family members? How do you feel about the grumpy old man who lives next door? It's a little easier to love people half way around the world than it is to love the ones you see all the time.

Over and over in the Bible we are told to love one another. The people you see every day are the ones who need your love the most.

Dear Lord,

Some of the people around me are so hard to love. I'm gonna need Your help with this.

Amen

Calm Faith

Relaxing in the Lord. That's what these verses teach. When you feel safe and secure you don't have to worry about anything. You know that someone is taking care of you and that everything will work out just fine.

If you're going to feel that way about anyone, it should be the Lord. He's watching over your life. That means He knows everything you do. Nothing surprises Him.

So, relax in Him and let Him direct you into the person He wants you to be.

Dear Lord,

I want to be able to trust You with everything. Help me learn to know that everything that happens to me is under Your control. *Amen*

THE **LORD** WILL KEEP YOU FROM ALL HARM — HE WILL **WATCH** OVER YOUR LIFE; THE LORD WILL WATCH OVER **YOUR COMING** AND GOING BOTH NOW AND **FOREVERMORE.**

PSALM 121:7-8

Work At It

ALWAYS GIVE
YOURSELVES
FULLY TO THE
WORK OF THE
LORD,

BECAUSE
YOU KNOW THAT YOUR
LABOR IN THE
LORD IS NOT
IN VAIN.

I CORINTHIANS 15:58

An Olympic level gymnast doesn't just practice ten minutes a day. A concert pianist sits down and tickles the ivory more often than once or twice a week. To get really good at something, you have to give yourself to it – devote your life to it.

Becoming the person God desires for you to be is a full-time job. Full time in the sense that you spend time with Him every day and you think about what He wants for you.

Keep working for Him and learning from Him. Don't let anything move you away from that!

Dear Lord,

I do want my life to count for You. Help me push other things aside and be devoted to You.

Amen

Wait - It's Worth It!

We live in a loose society. Some people think you're totally weird if you don't have a boyfriend. But the Bible teaches you to keep yourself pure. Rather wait for the right guy before you start dating left and right. Don't give in to peer pressure just because you want to be accepted and liked.

Likewise, it is good and honorable to wait for a new outfit, book, pair of shoes. This makes us appreciate things more. Waiting and saving for something teaches us patience and appreciation.

Dear Lord,

Help me to remember that waiting for something is more worthwhile than getting what I want right now.

Amen

KEEP yourself PURE.

I TIMOTHY 5:22

A New You

DO NOT LIE

to each other,

SINCE YOU HAVE TAKEN

OFF YOUR OLD SELF

WITH ITS PRACTICES

AND HAVE PUT ON

the new self,

WHICH IS BEING

renewed.

COLOSSIANS
3:9-10

Hey ... you're a new person. You received a new heart when you asked Jesus to come into your life. You're working with new equipment here so you have a chance to see new results and become a better you.

You're going to have to make some choices though. Satan is going to keep pounding away at you, trying to make you live the way you used to. Don't let him succeed!

Choose to keep your new heart activated so you don't lie to others and you don't keep doing the bad things you used to do ... the things that do not please God.

Dear Lord,

Help me to live like a new person and to stop doing the things I used to do. I don't have to do those things anymore. I want to please You.

Amen

Words and Reactions

It's so nice on a cold night to sit in front of the fireplace and enjoy a warm fire. When the flames begin to die down and you take the poker and stir them up a bit, maybe toss another log on the fire, what happens? The flames shoot back up and burn strong.

Did you know that your words and reactions have that same kind of power? When there is a conflict with a family member or friend, a kind, gentle answer can keep the flames of anger from shooting up. But if you start yipping at the other person with harsh words the flames will shoot up strong ... and probably burn for a while.

Keep your responses gentle and you'll keep the flames away.

Dear Lord,

Please help me control my reactions and my words. Guess I'm kind of a word firefighter, huh?

Amen

A gentle answer turns away wrath, but a harsh word stirs up anger.

Proverbs 15:1

A Jesus Attitude

IN YOUR RELATIONSHIP
**WITH
ONE ANOTHER,**
HAVE THE SAME
**MINDSET AS
CHRIST JESUS...**
HE MADE
HIMSELF
NOTHING BY TAKING THE
NATURE
OF A SERVANT.

PHILIPPIANS 2:5, 7

Some people need to be in charge. They want to be the most important, make all the decisions, and not do any dirty work. Yeah, some jobs are just below them.

Well, if you have that kind of attitude you're not reflecting Christ. Does this make sense – Jesus is the Son of God ... the Creator of the universe. But He didn't have to be the most important guy in the crowd. He came to serve others. He even washed His disciples' feet. That's about the lowest job He could have done. But He wanted to meet other people's needs and do whatever He could for them.

That's the way Jesus wants you to be, too.

Dear Lord,

Serving others is not what I want to do. Please help me to have an attitude like Jesus. *Amen*

Be Careful What You Say

Do you know the old saying, "Sticks and stones may break my bones, but words can never hurt me"? Yeah, it's not true. Words do hurt. Unkind words just lay inside a person like a ten pound pancake.

The way you talk to others shows what's in your heart. Your words should show what makes you different from people who don't know Christ.

Let your words be filled with grace and kindness. Don't hurt others by what you say – even if you're just joking around. Sometimes your efforts to make your friends laugh are at the expense of another person.

Dear Lord,

I like to make my friends laugh. But I don't want to do it by making fun of someone else or hurting anyone. Help me to be careful what I say.

Amen

LET YOUR CONVERSATION BE ALWAYS FULL OF grace, SEASONED WITH SALT, SO THAT YOU MAY know how TO ANSWER EVERYONE.

COLOSSIANS 4:6

No-Whine Zone

Do everything without grumbling or arguing, so that you... shine like stars in the universe.

Philippians 2:14-15

Okay, you've asked Jesus to come into your life and you're doing pretty good at having devotions, praying, attending church and youth group. It looks like things are going pretty well. But how are you doing in the no complaining or arguing category of your life?

Complaining comes so naturally to some people – whining about other people; about jobs you are told to do; about responsibilities; about lack of freedom. And arguing, well, family relationships and friendships are nearly impossible without some arguing.

But, what's going to make you stand out from others – shine like a star – is if you *don't* do those things. That shows that Christ is in your life!

Dear Lord,

Complaining and arguing come so naturally to me. You're going to have to help me with this.

Amen

Don't Envy

*W*anting what someone else has only leads to trouble. If you let your thoughts linger on that "want," pretty soon it's all you can think about. You want your friend's clothes, house, "stuff," talents, maybe even her parents and before you know it, your friendship with her is shot.

Envy destroys everything around it. It seeps into all your attitudes. It wrecks friendships and relationships with your own family or friends – anyone you feel may be holding you back from having what you want.

Don't let envy take control of your mind, after all, who wants to have rotten bones? Be at peace with what you have and who you are!

Dear God,

This is hard. There is stuff I want but don't have. Help me to be content with who I am and what I have.

Amen

A heart at peace gives life to the body, but envy rots the bones. Proverbs 14:30

Heart Focus

"WHERE YOUR TREASURE IS, THERE YOUR HEART WILL BE ALSO."

MATTHEW 6:21

What's the most important thing in your life right now? Friends? Music? Sports? Are you not sure how to answer that question? Well, on what do you spend most of your time and energy? Bingo! That's where your treasure is.

You may think that your heart is focused on one thing – knowing and serving God or even your family – but if your time doesn't go to that, then you're just fooling yourself.

What does it mean that your heart is in the same place as your treasure? Well, think about it. Whatever your time and thoughts are focused on is quickly going to become the most important thing in your life. Make sure your heart is focused on something worthwhile!

Dear Lord,

The most worthwhile thing I can think of is You. Help me to focus on You! *Amen*

We Need Each Other

*P*eople need each other. God created us to live in community with others. You know that sometimes life is hard and you get tired and discouraged. It means a lot when a friend comes along with a word of encouragement. That kind word may be what keeps you going for another few days. You can be an encourager for other people, too. When you see someone who needs encouragement or just needs a friend, be there for her!

Take time to encourage others every day. Sometimes it's a friend, sometimes a family member who will need your encouragement. Help anyone who is struggling. You'll have the joy of helping someone you love or of making a new friend!

Dear Lord,

Help me pay attention to those around me. Help me be there for anyone who may need my help.

Amen

Hebrews 3:13

Peacefulness

Turn from evil and do good; seek peace & pursue it.

Psalm 34:14

What kind of image does the word *peace* bring into your mind? A big field of tall grass gently blowing in the breeze? Maybe a tiny baby quietly sleeping? How about a beautiful sunset over a smooth lake?

Images of peace don't often include things like a stock car race. What does personal peace look like, or more realistically, what does it feel like? Quiet, trusting, with no anxiety and no fear.

God wants His children to pursue that kind of peace – look for it and try to make it a part of your life. Peace like that sets God's children apart from the rest of the world.

Dear Lord,

I think it must be important that this verse says to turn away from evil before looking for peace. Help me to do good and seek peace. Amen

Life Lessons

Why do teachers have to give us so much homework? It really gets old, doesn't it? Of course the reason you have homework is to help you learn – it works even if you don't think so. Well, if you want to learn to become a better person, it makes sense that you will have to let God teach you.

Sometimes lessons are hard, but they are helping you learn how to live with other people and be kind and loving.

God's lessons help you learn how to obey Him and serve Him, too. God's lessons, your homework, is to read His Word and talk with Him.

Dear God,

I do want to learn new things so I guess if I have to do homework, I will. Help me learn quickly. *Amen*

TEACH ME YOUR WAYS so I may know You and continue to FIND FAVOR with You.

Exodus 33:13

Road Maps

ASK WHERE THE GOOD WAY IS, & walk IN IT, AND you WILL find REST FOR YOUR SOULS. JEREMIAH 6:16

There's an old joke that says that men will always refuse to ask directions, no matter how lost they are. Of course, it isn't fair, but there is a lesson in this. If you don't know where you're going, you can wander around in circles for a long, long time without ever getting to where you want to go. You waste a lot of time that way. You don't want to do that in your life.

But how do you find out where you should be going? You need a life map with the roads clearly marked. Ask God to show you. He will – then, read His Word for further directions.

Most importantly, when you know which way to go – do it!

Dear Lord,

Help me to find the right way and to follow it closely! *Amen*

Waiting Patiently

Waiting is one of the hardest things in the world. Waiting to grow up, waiting to drive, waiting to date, waiting for your dreams to come true. You can learn a lot of lessons while you're waiting though.

If you don't rush ahead into life, but wait for God to teach you and show you what He wants for you, you might be surprised at what you learn. You'll only hear His quiet voice in your heart when you're still.

Rushing around like crazy will definitely cut into your learning. God won't make you sit down and wait to hear His voice. He wants it to be your choice.

Dear God,

It's hard to sit down and just be still. There is always something to do. Help me learn to be still before You.   *Amen*

WAIT FOR THE LORD; BE STRONG AND TAKE HEART AND WAIT FOR THE LORD.

PSALM 27:14

Good Forgiveness

Bear with each other & forgive one another if any of you has a grievance against someone. Forgive as the Lord forgave you.

Colossians 3:13

You're not going to get anywhere in your Christian life if you don't learn to forgive others. After all, God has forgiven you for the wrong things you've done – learn from that and be willing to forgive others.

Being able to forgive, even really mean things, will show that you have God's love in you.

Forgiving isn't easy – it's easier to be angry or hold a grudge. But you can be better than that.

When you're angry with someone, forgiving them shows how far you've come in your walk with God. It is the best you possible!

Dear God,

Help me be more forgiving. Help me remember how often You forgive me for the things I do.

Amen

Be Like Christ

If you keep on doing what you do, you'll continue to get what you got. For example, if you eat junk food all the time, you're gonna be overweight. If you read comic books non-stop, you'll never learn your school lessons.

In the same way, change what you put into your mind if you want to have different actions come out. What you put in your mind and heart will become visible in how you live and how you treat others.

Make good choices, spend time with God's Word, ask God to teach you with His wisdom. Seek to become that kind, considerate person who shows God's love to everyone around her. Stand out from the crowd – be more Christlike.

Dear Lord,

I do want to be more like Christ. Teach me. Please show me how!

Amen

The **WISDOM** from **ABOVE** is first **PURE**, then peaceable, **GENTLE** ... impartial & **SINCERE**.

JAMES 3:17

Loving Others

Anyone who LOVES their *brother* & *sister* lives in the LIGHT, and there is nothing in them to make them stumble.

1 John 2:10

One command that's given over and over in the Bible is: "Love one another." When you're around friends who like to talk about other people, it's a real temptation to join right in with them. It can get to be such a habit that you don't even realize you're doing it. That is NOT showing love.

Another thing that happens is that your group can become so close that other girls aren't accepted. They're always left on the outside – a lonely place to be.

Becoming the young woman God wants you to be will mean that you are loving to all those around you. That will set you apart from others.

Dear Lord,

I've never thought about how other kids might feel if they're not accepted into my group of friends. Help me to be loving and to encourage my friends to be loving, too. *Amen*

Differences

How do you feel about kids who are "different" from you? Do deaf or blind people make you uncomfortable? How about kids in wheel chairs – especially those who have diseases that make it difficult for them to speak or control their hand movements.

Yeah, they are different, but that doesn't give you the right to give them a hard time or make fun of them ... or ignore them.

Take the time to get to know someone who is different. You might discover a really wonderful person. And you might give a lonely person the gift of friendship!

Dear God,

Some people kind of scare me. But, I want to get past that. Give me the courage to start a conversation with someone who is different from me.

Amen

"Do not curse the deaf or put a stumbling block in front of the blind, **BUT** **FEAR YOUR GOD. I AM THE LORD.**"

LEVITICUS 19:14

All Are Gifted

We have different **GIFTS,** according to the **GRACE GIVEN TO EACH OF US.**

Romans 12:6

"I wish I could play the piano like Sarah does." "I wish I could do gymnastics like Mallory." "I wish I had straight blond hair like Cori." "Why can't I talk with new people like Joy does?"

Are you always comparing yourself to other girls ... and feeling as if you come up short? Well ... *stop it.* God gave each person different gifts, and He gave *all* of us gifts. We're all different, but we all need to work together to make God's family the best it can be. Don't wish your life away by wanting the gifts someone else has.

Ask God to show you what gifts He has given you – what you're good at and what you enjoy. Then go to work developing those gifts to become the best you possible!

Dear Lord,

Show me what my gifts are. Help me learn to use them every day – for You! *Amen*

Get Excited

Zeal ... that's not a word you hear a lot anymore. What does it mean? Energy, enthusiasm, passion. In other words – you feel zeal for things you are really excited about. Is there anything in your life that you have zeal for? Not just zeal for a minute or two, but real zeal that consumes your thoughts and energy? Maybe you aren't zealous about anything right now.

Well, God doesn't want any of His children to be lukewarm about their faith or about serving Him. He wants your zeal! Get excited about what God has done for you. Get excited about how much He loves you. Get excited about His plans for your life. Don't let anything spoil your excitement.

Dear God,

I didn't even know what zeal meant before this. But I want to have zeal for You! Help me to get excited about You!

Amen

Never be lacking in zeal, but keep your spiritual fervor, serving the Lord.

Romans 12:11

The Best Life Ever

FOR TO **ME,** TO **LIVE** IS **CHRIST** AND TO DIE IS **GAIN.**

PHILIPPIANS 1:21

*P*retty serious verse. What's it saying? That the most important thing in life is to glorify Christ. What does that mean? Glorifying Christ is when everything in your life is for Him and points to Him.

It's done by obeying God – living by the standards of His Word. It's done by giving Him credit for your life and by recognizing His creative power.

What does the second part of this verse mean – dying is gain? It means that heaven is God's gift to His children. Heaven is a more wonderful place than can ever be imagined! There's no sadness, no sin, no problems, just wonderful time with God. Knowing that heaven is in your future is awesome!

Dear God,

Making Jesus the focus of my life and living for Him every day ... well, I have a ways to go. Please help me.

Amen

Don't Toot Your Own Horn

Everyone knows one. Every crowd has one – that one person who brags about everything she does.

That one person who thinks she is better, smarter, prettier and more important than anyone else. Those kinds of people aren't much fun to be around, are they? Truth is, they don't please God much either. He's more kind toward humble people. People who lift up others, encouraging them to be the best people they can be.

Braggy people lift themselves up by pushing other people down. That stinks. Don't toot your own horn – if you do, then your song may not be worth playing.

Dear God,

Help me remember this every time I'm tempted to brag about myself. Help me to see the good things in other people and to encourage them.

Amen

Clothe yourselves, all of you, with humility toward one another.

1 PETER 5:5

Hopefulness

PUT YOUR **HOPE** IN GOD. FOR I WILL YET PRAISE HIM, MY SAVIOR AND MY GOD.
PSALM 42:5

*W*here's your hope? The thing you think is going to pull you through when the going gets tough. There are so many things in this world that claim to be worthy of your hope. But are they? Friends are good, wonderful even, but are they worthy of putting your hope in?

Popularity, money, success, fame, these are all things that claim they are worthy of your hope. But, are they? Would those things actually be able to help you in a crisis? Are they worth giving all of your time and energy to? No way!

The only person worthy of your hope is God! Be different from the world. Put your hope in God only. Live for Him and praise Him!

Dear God,

Thank You for loving me. Thank You for all You give me. I praise You with all my heart.

Amen

Truth First

"You're my best friend." When you hear those words from someone you really care about, then find out that she didn't mean it at all ... well, it really hurts.

No one likes to be lied to. Not even those little white lies like, "Yeah, your hair looks good that way," when it really looks like a floor mop gone wild.

Lies hurt. Becoming the best person you can be means stopping the lies. Don't even tell the "I-don't-want-to-hurt-your-feelings-so-I'm-just-gonna-fudge-a-little" kind of lies. It is possible to be honest and kind at the same time. Show enough respect for your family and friends to tell them the truth.

Dear God,

I hate it when someone lies to me. I don't want to hurt my friends that way. Help me always tell the truth and to find a kind way to do that.

Amen

DO NOT DECEIVE ONE ANOTHER.

LEVITICUS 19:11

To Sum It Up!

Let love & FAITHFULNESS NEVER LEAVE you; BIND THEM *around your neck,* *write them* **ON THE TABLET** *of your heart.* Proverbs 3:3

What have you learned about becoming the best you ever? There's two pretty basic foundations to that happening. Number one is to love God and love others. God's Word says over and over again to love Him and to love others. It says it a lot, so it must be important.

The second thing is to trust God. Believe who He is and what He has done for you. You can't really love Him if you don't trust Him. You can't live your life for Him if you don't love Him. There's a chain reaction here.

Now, how do you grow more in love with God and learn to trust Him more? Simple ... read His Word. Talk with Him. Ask Him for His Spirit's help.

Dear God,

You want me to be the best person I can be. That's why I know You will help me. Let's get going!

Amen

Praise God!

Have you ever gone to a high school football or basketball game? Did you enjoy watching the cheerleaders who try to get the crowd excited about the game by leading cheers? They do amazing routines, sometimes even tossing one another into the air. Their energy and enthusiasm is contagious. Praising God is like being a cheerleader for Him.

Moses' words of praise are recorded in Exodus and he couldn't say enough good things about God!

Praising God can be done privately and publicly. Praising God means recognizing all the wonderful things He is and does!

Dear God,

I want to praise You, too! Thank You for putting prayers like this one in the Bible so I can see how others have praised You through the years!

Amen

Thanks for the Good Times

Sometimes life is crummy – there are those times when it seems like absolutely *nothing* is going right. When most people have trouble in their lives they cry out to God for help. People expect God to do something for them when they have a crisis. They are also ready to blame Him for some of the problems in their lives.

But, when things are going well, do those same people remember to praise God for His gifts and for the good times in their lives? Mmm – sometimes, but not nearly enough.

Remember to turn to God for help. He wants to help you. But don't forget to praise Him when things are going well! He also wants to know that you appreciate His care.

Dear God,

Thank You for the good times in my life. They make the hard times easier to handle. *Amen*

IS ANYONE AMONG YOU IN TROUBLE? LET THEM PRAY.

IS ANYONE HAPPY? LET THEM SING SONGS OF PRAISE.
JAMES 5:13

Hope Equals Praise

Now there is in store for me the crown OF righteousness, which the Lord, the righteous Judge, will award to me on that day.

◊ 2 TIMOTHY 4:8 ◊

*G*od promises hope – a crown of righteousness – that's in heaven! You see, even if you have spent most of your life just doing your own thing and not caring a bit about what God wants – even if you have deliberately disobeyed God and flat-out turned your back on Him – you can have hope.

That's 'cause God looks at your heart, and He sees if you have a longing for Him, a longing for Christ to come back, a longing to obey and please God.

He sees what your real desires are and He gives you a chance to change.

Dear God,

Thank You for looking at my heart instead of at the stupid things I do all the time. I do want to obey You and I praise You for giving me chance after chance!

Amen

Praise God for Creation!

God spent six busy days making everything there is on this earth ... including the earth itself. He's the reason you have anything to enjoy, anything to do, anyone to love. All He had to do was say a word and things started happening. Nothing that God made was by accident. He thought about what He was making and after He made it all, He looked at it and decided He had done a good job. Things turned out the way He wanted.

Praise God for thinking of everything in this world. Praise Him for caring about what you would enjoy. Praise Him for paying attention to detail. Praise Him for making this great big wonderful world!

Dear God,

Sometimes I take Your creation for granted. I am thankful for this world. It's beautiful. You did a great job!

Amen

GOD SAW everything that HE had MADE, AND BEHOLD, it was VERY GOOD.

GENESIS 1:31

White as Snow

"Though your sins are like *Scarlet,* they shall be as *white as snow.*"

Isaiah 1:18

If you've ever spilled spaghetti sauce on a white sweater you know that a red stain is *hard* to get out. You can scrub and scrub and use all kinds of special treatments, but it's very hard to get rid of the spot. Even when you've washed it over and over and no one else can see the stain – you still can 'cause you know where it is.

Well, that's kind of how your sins are to God's pureness. Like a bright red stain that only fades to pink. But Jesus' death on the cross took care of the stain. Because of Him your sins are *gone* – you look white as snow now! Praise God for that!

Dear God,

Wow! Thank You so much. What a wonderful plan to get rid of the sin stain on my heart. You're awesome!

Amen

Heartfelt Praise

Praise cannot be half-hearted. It's not one of those things that you can "sort of" do. The psalmist knew that and he committed to praising God with all his heart. He even told God how he would praise Him – by telling about all of God's wonders. That could be things like how a bird flies, how a butterfly begins life as a caterpillar, or why the ocean stays within the boundaries God made for it.

You might tell of the wonder that God loves you, not only you, but all the people who ever lived. Maybe the wonder that fascinates you is the hope of being in heaven for eternity! Whatever it is, praise God loud and clear for it.

Dear God,

It's good to think about Your wonders and which of them is most important to me! I thank You and praise You for them all. Amen

I WILL give thanks TO YOU, LORD, WITH ALL MY heart; I WILL TELL OF ALL YOUR wonderful DEEDS.

PSALM 9:1

Focus on God

My eyes **are ever** on the **LORD.**
• • • PSALM 25:15 • • •

When you start learning to drive you'll find out that more often than not, wherever you're looking is where the car will be going.

Of course, when you're driving that's good motivation for keeping your eyes on the road – otherwise your teacher will scream a lot!

This carries through to your Christian life. As long as you keep your eyes firmly on God, you'll be fine. But, if you let your eyes wander to other things – popularity, boys, fashion, even self-centeredness – anything that pulls you away from God, well, you're gonna have trouble.

Dear God,

I praise You for helping me all the time! Help me keep my eyes on You. I want to stay focused and not be tempted to put too much importance on the wrong things. *Amen*

Always the Same

There are a million things to praise God for. One major thing, though, would be His constancy. What does that mean? It means that Jesus is never in a bad mood. He's never out to make you look bad while He looks good.

You know when you go to Him in prayer that He is going to be exactly the same today as He was yesterday and will be tomorrow. Jesus' purpose is to help you know God and grow closer and closer to Him.

You'll always get what you expect when you go to God.

Dear God,

There's a lot of comfort in that. I know that You always love me, always consider certain things sin and are pleased with other things ... always.

Amen

JESUS CHRIST is the SAME YESTERDAY & TODAY & FOREVER.

Hebrews 13:8

He Hears, Cares and Acts

I SOUGHT THE LORD, AND HE ANSWERED ME; HE DELIVERED ME FROM ALL MY FEARS.

PSALM 34:4

"My hero!" That's what the damsels in distress would say to their rescuers in the old movies. When someone saves you from danger he becomes your hero and you shower him with thanks and usually tell others about his good deeds.

Have you turned to God when you were afraid and only later realized that He helped you through the difficult situation?

Did you realize that He not only helped you – He heard your prayer and cared about what you were facing? That's certainly something to praise God for. He hears. He cares. He acts. Praise God!

Dear Father,

I am so thankful that You hear my prayers and that You answer them. Thank You! *Amen*

The Holy Spirit Helps

A familiar scene in old movies would be when the good guys are outnumbered by the bad guys. The battle is raging on and it looks pretty hopeless for the good guys. But, suddenly, the cavalry rides in! They fight off the bad guys and save the day for the good guys!

Ah ... if only life were like the movies. Well, maybe it is! You don't have to fight off the bad guy by yourself, either. Here's the scoop – when you gave your life to Jesus, you became His child and He will help you guard your heart.

The Holy Spirit will ride over the hill and fight off whoever and whatever is threatening you – just call on Him! Praise God for the cavalry!

Dear God,

It's awesome to know that I'm not alone. Thanks for the Holy Spirit and all His help. *Amen*

Guard the good deposit that was entrusted to you – guard it with the help of the Holy Spirit who lives in us.

2 Timothy 1:14

Amazing Forgiveness!

YOU ARE A God READY TO forgive, gracious AND merciful.

NEHEMIAH 9:17

*P*raise God for His forgiveness. That's something He has to do over and over for most of us.

Stop and think about how hurt and angry you feel toward a friend who hurts your feelings – especially if it was on purpose! It's hard to forgive – especially more than once! Really think about the act of forgiving. It's hard, isn't it?

Now, do you realize how incredible it is that God is willing to forgive you over and over and over! He loves you that much!

Take time to thank Him ... not just thank Him ... but praise Him for His forgiveness!

Dear God,

I don't deserve it. You forgive my mistakes and my selfish acts over and over. I just don't deserve it. But I sure am thankful! *Amen*

Close to You

Movie stars, athletes, politicians all travel with an entourage. That means it's nearly impossible to get close to them. If you wait for hours in a crowd to see your favorite singer, you'll probably have to look through a crowd of bodyguards to get a glimpse of him or her. Seems that if famous people are that hard to get close to, then it would be nearly impossible to get close to God – the Creator of *everything*. Well, praise Him 'cause that's not true!

It is so amazing – God, the Creator of the universe; God who hears the prayers of all mankind; God who deals with all kinds of natural disasters and really *serious* stuff is near to little ole you. He loves you.

Dear God,

Every time I think about it I'm amazed that even with all the major stuff You have to take care of, You care about me too. Thank You.

Amen

THE LORD is near to all who call on Him, to all who call on Him in truth.

Psalm 145:18

Light in Darkness

GOD IS light in Him THERE IS NO DARKNESS.

1 JOHN 1:5

*H*ave you ever tried to find your way through a room when it is dark; so dark that you can't even see your own hand in front of your face? Pretty scary, huh? Trying to walk when you can't tell if there is something solid to put your foot on is unnerving.

Growing up feels like that sometimes. There are so many choices to make about what kind of person you're going to be and what are the right things to do. The options pulling at you make it feel like you're walking in total darkness and the right path is lost.

The Hope – the Light – is God. Seek Him and the right path will light up for you. Maybe not as bright as an airport runway, but you will be able to see it in the darkness.

Dear Lord,

I praise You for being the Light. Your light helps me find my way in the dark times of life.

Amen

Amazing Love

Ahhh, sweet love. Be honest now, is there some guy that you spend time daydreaming about? Thinking about how it would be to know that he loved you? Everyone wants to be loved. Everyone wants to know they are special to someone. There's nothing wrong with that. But, in the middle of that daydreaming, don't forget that there is already Someone who loves you more than you can imagine (Someone besides your family).

The words from John 15 were spoken by Jesus. Think about what He's saying – in the same way that His Father loves Him, He loves you! That's complete, total, no-holds-barred love! Love that watches out for you, cares about you, will never, never fade away. Amazing!

Dear God,

It's hard to comprehend that You love me that much! I'm so thankful You do. I praise You for Your amazing love!

Amen

"As the Father has loved Me, so I have loved you."

John 15:9

Love in Action

HE POURED
WATER
INTO A
BASIN
AND BEGAN TO
WASH HIS
DISCIPLES' FEET,
DRYING
THEM WITH A
TOWEL THAT WAS
WRAPPED
AROUND HIM.

JOHN 13:5

Jesus didn't just teach with words. He also taught by example. He wanted His disciples to understand how important it is to do things for others that aren't easy; things that some people think they're too good to do.

Washing feet was a job that servants usually did. It was something that one of His disciples should have done for Him ... but none of them did.

God put stories like this in the Bible to show that sometimes it's important to get your hands dirty and do the jobs that no one else wants to do. Do something for someone else that shows them how important they are to you. Follow Jesus' example and remember to praise Him for being that example!

Dear God,

I do praise You for examples like this. Please help me, I will try my best to follow Your example.

Amen

Reach Out and Touch

*R*each out and touch someone," used to be the advertising slogan of a big telephone company. People long to be touched. The human touch conveys love and acceptance. Look at what Jesus did – a man with leprosy came to Him and asked to be healed.

Leprosy is a highly contagious disease and is spread through touching the sores of a leper. In Jesus' day, lepers had to live away from their families and NO ONE wanted to touch them. Jesus could have healed the man with just a word or even a thought. He didn't have to touch him, but He did. Praise God that He cares enough to reach out and touch you. That's real love!

Dear God,

Thanks for loving me that much. What Jesus did helps me know that You'll never turn away from me.

Amen

Jesus WAS INDIGNANT. HE REACHED out & TOUCHED THE MAN.

Mark 1:41

He Cares

LUKE 7:13

WHEN THE LORD SAW HER, HIS HEART WENT OUT TO HER AND HE SAID, "Don't cry."

It might be easy to think that God is so busy with the "big" stuff of this world that He doesn't really have time to care about the things that weigh down our hearts. But, that's just not true. God cares when your heart is hurting.

Jesus met a woman who was a widow – the only family she had left in the world was her son who had just died. She was on her way to bury the boy when Jesus met her.

Read the verse again – His heart went out to her. Jesus cared about her pain. If He cared about her pain, you can know that He cares about yours, too! Praise Him for caring when your heart hurts!

Dear God,

I am thankful for Your care. It is amazing to know that You care when my heart is hurting!

Amen

No Excuses

You try to tell your teacher, "Uhhh, I didn't know there was gonna be a test." Nope, won't work 'cause she knows that means you didn't pay attention. You can tell your parents, "Uhhh, I didn't know I was supposed to clean my room." Nope, won't work either 'cause you're not new to the house rules.

You can even try telling God, "Uhhh, I didn't know You'd help me." Nope, won't work 'cause here's the promise that He will. All you have to do is ask and God will give you what you need. Look for Him and you will find Him.

Do you get it – He *wants* to help you, but He wants you to ask Him for His help. How awesome is that? God Himself wants you to ask Him for help!

Dear God,

Thank You, thank You, thank You. It's amazing that You love me that much!

Amen

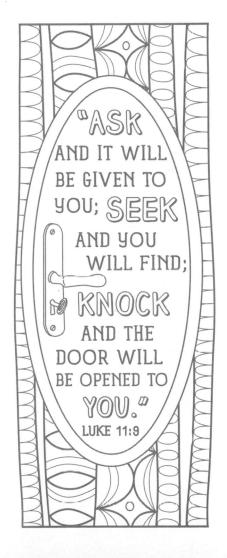

"ASK AND IT WILL BE GIVEN TO YOU; SEEK AND YOU WILL FIND; KNOCK AND THE DOOR WILL BE OPENED TO YOU."

LUKE 11:9

The Most Wonderful Gift

He SAVED US, not because of works done by us in righteousness, but according to His own mercy.

TITUS 3:5

Think you're pretty cool, do ya? Think you've got your act together and you're in the "coolest" group? Think you're just a bit better than some other kids? Well ... get over yourself. The most awesome thing that has or ever will happen to you, you had absolutely nothing to do with.

The highest status you could ever achieve is being a member of God's family. That happened when you were saved – and being saved is something you definitely did not deserve.

God saved you just because He loves you, not because you earned it. Praise Him for your salvation – the most wonderful gift that was completely undeserved.

Dear Father,

I am so thankful for Your awesome salvation. You're amazing!

Amen

Handmade

Have you ever worked very hard to make something? Maybe you made some pottery, painted a picture, wrote a story ... whatever it was ... you were incredibly proud and protective of it, right? You wanted others to respect it and be careful with it.

Well, put yourself right there in that category. You are God's workmanship. He created you and He is very protective of you. He wants others ... and you, yourself, to be careful with you.

You were created with a purpose in mind. How awesome is that? You can do something for God – a job He planned just for you.

Dear God,

It is totally amazing that You made me and You are proud of what You made! It is also very exciting that there is a job I can do for You!

Amen

WE ARE HIS WORKMANSHIP, CREATED IN Christ Jesus FOR GOOD WORKS.
EPHESIANS 2:10

A New You

2 Corinthians 5:17

IF ANYONE IS IN CHRIST, HE IS A NEW creation.

Okay, this is pretty gross, but did you know that snakes shed their skins and grow new ones? Yeah, they just crawl right out of the old ones and within a few days they have new skin. How cool is that?

Can you crawl out of your skin? You kind of can. When you asked Jesus into your life, He made you brand new. The old you – the one that doesn't pay any attention to God and just does what she wants – is gone.

In its place is the new you – the one who cares about God and wants to obey Him and live the life He wants you to live. How cool is *that*? You are a new you, because of Christ.

Dear God,

That is so awesome. Thank You for making me new ... completely new! *Amen*

Always Available

When you need extra math help from your teacher, do you have to make an appointment to see her? You can't just drop in at her house on a Sunday afternoon, right? What about a dentist appointment? You've got a terrible toothache but you can't see your dentist until a week from Tuesday ... that's a bummer.

Here's something cool – you don't have to make an appointment to meet with God. He doesn't have strict office hours between 9 and 5. He's available to you every single day, in fact, every moment of every day and night.

He's there to help you with your problems, to lift them off your shoulders and take care of them for you.

Dear Lord,

I'm so thankful that I can come to You any time of the day or night and know that You're there. Thank You so much. *Amen*

Praise be to the Lord, to God our Savior, who daily bears our burdens.
Psalm 68:19

Unchanging Love

1 John 4:16

*T*here are not many absolutely sure things in this world, things that you can trust all the time. Friends fail you once in a while and stuff certainly breaks down.

The one thing you can count on every single time is God's love for you. When everything else falls away; when you're feeling totally and completely alone, you can count on the fact that God is there ... loving you like always. His constant love is a foundation that you can build the rest of your life on.

Praise Him for His love; His constant, pure, unfailing love. Love that never changes. You can always count on God's love.

Dear God,

I do praise You for Your love. I know I'm not always easy to love, but You do it. Thanks.

Amen

Strength and Peace

"It's too hard. I can't do it!" Ever said that? About what? Math, gym class, being nice to someone who was mean to you? Everyone faces hard things – different things for everyone – but hard none the less.

Did you know you have a secret weapon you can call on? A secret weapon? Yes – God. You don't have to face hard stuff alone. God's strength that created the universe, parted the waters of the Red Sea and raised Jesus back to life – that's the strength available to you.

All you have to do is ask Him. He's waiting to help you. Of course, when you have that strength in your life, peace comes right along with it.

Dear Lord,

Thank You for Your strength and peace. I'm so thankful that You are in my life. *Amen*

The Lord gives strength to His people; the Lord blesses His people with peace.

Psalm 29:11

An Example to Follow

CHRIST suffered FOR YOU, leaving you an EXAMPLE, that you should FOLLOW IN HIS STEPS.

1 PETER 2:21

Things are easier to do if you have an example to follow. When you're making a new recipe, it's easier if there are pictures. When you're learning a new game, instructions help. If you're learning a new trick in gymnastics, having someone show it to you can really help a lot.

Living the Christian life – the way God wants you to live – can be kind of confusing. So, it helps that you have an example to follow. Jesus walked on this earth, had choices to make, was tempted, had to deal with difficult people, had to choose to have prayer time – all the things you have to deal with. He left an example to follow. Be like Jesus and life will be much easier.

Dear Father,

Thank You for Jesus' example. It helps a lot to have someone to follow.

Amen

Your Bodyguard

*P*raise God for watching out for you! Absolutely nothing surprises Him. He knows every tough thing you have ever faced – or ever will. If your family is breaking up because your parents fight all the time – He knows. If someone you love is dying – He knows. If you're lonely – He knows.

Get this: *You are not alone.* He's with you in all those difficult situations and as tough as they are to go through, they won't kill you. He's your God and He's watching out for you. Hold tight to Him and praise Him for being with you.

Dear God,

Sometimes I'm scared. Sometimes I feel alone. Thank You for reminding me that You are with me and watching out for me always. *Amen*

"WHEN YOU PASS THROUGH THE WATERS, I WILL BE with you; AND THROUGH THE RIVERS, THEY SHALL NOT OVERWHELM YOU; WHEN YOU WALK THROUGH FIRE you SHALL NOT BE BURNED."

ISAIAH 43:2

Praise Him!

"THE PEOPLE I FORMED FOR MYSELF THAT THEY MAY PROCLAIM MY PRAISE."

Isaiah 43:21

God gives you so much – everything. He created this earth for you to live on and the sun to warm it. He filled the night sky with beautiful stars. He made oceans, mountains, rivers, flowers. He created butterflies and puppies and kittens and ponies. He made families to love you and care for you. He gave you friends to fill your life with laughter.

What other things can you add to this list? What is your response to all God has given you? He wants it to be praise for Him.

Celebrate His goodness and love by telling others about Him. Praise Him!

Dear Father,

I praise You for Your wonderful gifts. I praise You for Your care for me. I praise You for who You are!

Amen

Patience

Team try-outs can be so stressful. If you've ever tried out for a sports team, dance team or cheerleading squad you know how stressful it is. They have a certain number of slots to fill and everyone who tries out will not make the team. Truthfully, the coaches don't want everyone on the team. They want only those they consider to be the best.

Thank God that He isn't that way. He wants everyone to be part of His family. Praise Him for His patience – He's waiting for more and more people to come to Him. He wants everyone to be able to spend eternity with Him in heaven.

Dear Father,

I'm so thankful that You waited for me. I'm thankful that my family and friends who don't know You still have a chance to choose You!

Amen

He is patient with you, not wanting anyone to perish, but everyone to come to repentance.

2 Peter 3:9

Everlasting Love

THIS IS HOW GOD SHOWED HIS LOVE AMONG US: HE SENT HIS ONE AND ONLY SON INTO THE WORLD THAT WE MIGHT LIVE THROUGH HIM.

1 JOHN 4:9

The easy way to "show love" is to drop a few dollars into a jar to help victims of some disaster begin to rebuild their lives. Or, you can volunteer at your church.

But there is another, more personal way to show love and it is what God did for you. He gave you His most precious Son – His only Son. God certainly could have come up with a plan to save the world without giving up His Son.

But, He wanted us to *know* how *much* He loves us. Therefore He gave the One He loves the most.

Dear God,

I know You sent Jesus, but I never thought about how much love that shows me. Thank You for loving me so much! *Amen*

He Understands

Quit complaining about how tough your life is and how no one understands what you're dealing with. Jesus does. He spent forty days with Satan bombarding Him with temptation after temptation. He didn't eat or drink for that whole time. He was tired and weak and Satan never left Him alone.

He knows what temptation feels like. He knows that when you're tired, it's hard to fight it off. You can trust Him to help you, because He knows what you're going through.

Praise God for this plan. It means that Jesus can identify with your struggles. He can help because He understands.

Dear God,

I'm sure it was hard to let Jesus go through that — but thank You. It makes a difference that Jesus understands. *Amen*

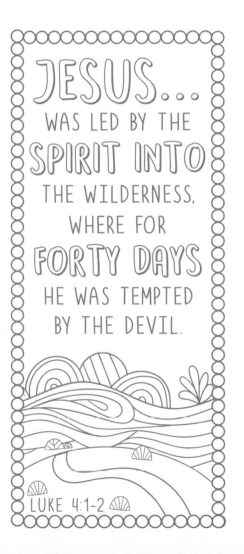

JESUS... WAS LED BY THE SPIRIT INTO THE WILDERNESS, WHERE FOR FORTY DAYS HE WAS TEMPTED BY THE DEVIL.

LUKE 4:1-2

Praise God

LET THEM PRAISE THE NAME OF the Lord, FOR HIS NAME ALONE is exalted; HIS SPLENDOR IS above the EARTH AND THE heavens.

PSALM 148:13

Get serious about praising God. Psalm 148 talks about all of creation praising Him. The oceans, skies, mountains and creatures all praise Him. Be honest with yourself now, how much time do you spend talking about your favorite band or movie star? How much of your conversation is about a cute boy?

God alone is worthy of your praise. Let Him hear it. Sing out your praises for His love, power, care, forgiveness and protection. Praise Him by the way you live your life. Praise Him to others. Praise Him always in all ways!

Dear Father,

I spend more time asking You for stuff than praising You. I'm sorry. I praise You for all You are and all You do! *Amen*

Number One!

"LOVE the Lord your God with all your heart and with all your SOUL and with all your mind. This is the first & GREATEST commandment."

MATTHEW 22:37-38

*D*o you ever wonder what is *really* important in life? After all, there are so many things thrown at you – especially from advertisers. "Get skinny!" "Wear this kind of jeans!" "Listen to this music!" Put things in perspective. Whatever you have been treating as the most important thing in the world is probably not.

It may be hard for you to believe that anything could be more important than being popular. But, these verses show that nothing should be more important to you than loving God completely. No one is saying that friends are not important, but keep them in perspective. When you love God with all your heart, soul and mind, nothing will come before Him.

Dear God,

Help me to get my priorities straight. I want You to be my top priority. *Amen*

Number Two Priority

When push comes to shove, most people will say that God is powerful and important. But, after God, what's in the number two spot? The Bible says number two is others.

Now, here's the weird part – loving others in the same way you love yourself.

What does that mean? Well, you take care of yourself, keep yourself safe, make yourself look good, in general, you look out for yourself. God says to do that for others, too, and not just your friends. He means even people you don't know well or people you don't especially like.

Hey, it's not easy ... but you can always ask God for help.

Dear God,

I'm going to need Your help! I know some people who aren't that easy to love.

Amen

"This is the **first & greatest** commandment. And the second is like it: 'Love your neighbor as yourself.'"

MATTHEW 22:38-39

A Good Thing

IT IS **good** to praise the LORD **& make music** to Your name, O Most High, proclaiming **Your love** in the morning and Your **faithfulness** at night.

PSALM 92:1-2

Okay, time to be honest with yourself — do you get tired of other (older) people constantly telling you what to do? Honestly, do you sometimes feel as though you don't have the opportunity to set your own priorities because someone else is doing it for you? Yeah, it does feel like that sometimes.

But one thing you do have control over is your heart. Even if others direct your time, they can't control what your heart feels. You must choose whether or not you will praise God.

Here's a chance to make a mature choice — begin and end your days by praising God. It's a good thing to do.

Dear God,

I want praise for You to be my first thought in the morning and the last one I have at night. Praise You!

Amen

Your Choice

What kind of music do you listen to? Come on, be honest, what are the words; what does the story lift up and honor?

Okay, what kinds of movies or TV shows do you watch? What's the message about lifestyles and choices? The world is busy bombarding you with junk ... sinful priorities.

If living for God and obeying Him is going to be a priority for you, you will have to *choose* it. Pay attention to what you learned in Sunday school and church. Choose to spend time reading His Word, listen to music about Him, talk with Him. It's going to have to be a choice ... your choice.

Dear God,

I never thought about what kind of stuff I put in my mind through music, movies and TV. I want to make You my priority. Give me strength to make that my choice. *Amen*

We must pay the most careful attention, therefore, to what we have HEARD, so that we do not drift away.

Hebrews 2:1

Trust in God

"DO NOT LET YOUR HEARTS BE TROUBLED. YOU BELIEVE IN GOD; BELIEVE ALSO IN ME."

JOHN 14:1

*A*re you thinking, "Don't let my heart be troubled? Whoever said that must be crazy." Think so? Well, then you're calling Jesus crazy. Yeah, He said this. He knew that your life would be tough sometimes.

Jesus understands people. He knew that you would put your hope for making things better in other people or in things. He wanted you to know that none of those things can give you peace. Only trust in Him can settle your troubled heart. It's not easy to switch your trust focus. But, you gotta start somewhere.

Believe that God knows what's going on. Believe that He can do something to help you. Trust Him to do it.

Dear God,

Help me to start placing my trust in You. I already know other things don't work. I want to learn to trust You.

Amen

Always Learning

From the first steps of a baby to the teen's independence, the world constantly changes. More freedom means more choices which calls for more teaching and guidance. You're growing up and the choices before you are more significant than they were when you were a child.

You're facing choices that range from fooling around with boys and smoking to the people you choose to hang out with, what you think about God, how you treat other people and your opinion of yourself.

The best place to go for guidance during this journey is the Lord. Ask His help. Put your hope in Him.

Dear God,

Seems like there is always something to learn. But I want to learn what You can teach me. Please, guide me.

Amen

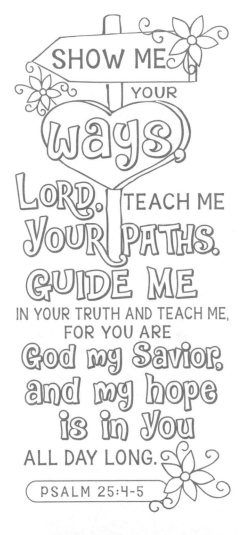

SHOW ME YOUR WAYS, LORD, TEACH ME YOUR PATHS. GUIDE ME IN YOUR TRUTH AND TEACH ME, FOR YOU ARE God my Savior, and my hope is in You ALL DAY LONG.

PSALM 25:4-5

God Equips You

Think about it – you walk into a dark room, flip a switch and the room is flooded with light. The light is always there, waiting for you to use it by flipping the switch.

In the same way, everything you need to live for God is right in front of you just waiting for you to access it. His instructions on how to live are in the Bible – everything you need to know to live a life of obedience.

And, if that's not enough, God is ready and waiting for you to talk to Him. He wants to guide you and show you what gifts and abilities He has given you. All you have to do is flip the switch to be equipped by Him.

Dear Father,

It's pretty exciting to think that You've given me everything I need to be able to do Your will. Help me find the "switch" and flip it on.

Amen

May the **GOD of peace...** equip you with everything **good** for doing **His will.**

Hebrews 13:20-21

Motive Check

Do your prayers have "I trouble"? Are they mostly what you want God to do for you? If so, you may need to change your style.

Talking to God about stuff that's important to you is what prayer is all about. But God is not a genie in a bottle to make you gorgeous, popular and rich.

Check your motives. Are you praying for things that will spread the message of His love to others? Are you asking Him to help you live in obedience to Him? If your prayers aren't being answered, it may be that your motives are wrong.

Dear Father,

Help me to examine my motives and make sure I'm asking for stuff for the right reasons. I want a powerful prayer life! *Amen*

When you ask, you do not receive, because you ASK with wrong motives, that you may spend what you get on your PLEASURES.

JAMES 4:3

Wearing Love

The fruit OF THE Spirit is love

GALATIANS 5:22

*A*re you a member of any kind of sports team or performing group? If so, you probably have a uniform to wear. When you come into a room and see someone in a uniform like yours, you know you're on the same team.

You're identifiable by your appearance. Well, that's true of a child of God, too. If you've asked Christ into your heart, His Spirit is living inside you and that will be evident by the love that flows from you.

The Spirit's love is the kind of love that gives others a chance, even if they are "different." It's a love that doesn't gossip or criticize. It's God's love and it comes from deep inside.

Are you identifiable by your love?

Dear Lord,

I'm good at loving my friends, but sometimes I'm not very loving to others. Fill me with Your love so people will know I'm Your child. *Amen*

Showing Joy

Do you know someone who always has a problem? Someone who constantly complains about stuff? Someone who looks at life with a "glass half-empty instead of half-full" viewpoint? It isn't much fun to be always around someone who is complaining. Hopefully that isn't you.

As a child of God, who has His Spirit living in your heart, one of the identifiable characteristics of your life should be joy. After all, you know God loves you. You know His power and guidance and that He is working in your life. You know that heaven is in your future. Why shouldn't you be joyful? Even when you have problems, you don't have to be hopeless.

Are you identifiable by your joy?

Dear Lord,

Don't let me get stuck in a complaining rut. Let me be joyous and share joy with others.

Amen

The fruit OF THE Spirit is LOVE, JOY

GALATIANS 5:22

A Peaceful Heart

The fruit
OF THE
Spirit is
LOVE, JOY,

peace

GALATIANS 5:22

"I'm scared of storms." "I worry about wars." "What if my parents split up?" When you think about it, there are all kinds of things to worry about. If you let your mind wander to all the things that *could* happen, you could spend a lot of time worrying. However, a heart filled with worry is the opposite of a heart filled with peace.

One characteristic of a heart where God's Spirit lives is peace. This heart knows that God is in control of everything – nothing surprises Him. No matter how bad things seem to be in the world or in your life, you can trust Him to take care of you and those you love. He never leaves you alone.

A heart that belongs to God is identifiable by peace.

Dear Father,

My life is not nearly as peaceful as I would like it to be. Help me learn to trust You more.

Amen

Patience Is a Virtue

"Why can't I date?" "I can't wait to get a driver's license." "It will be so cool when I can go to college." "I just want to move out on my own ..." Impatience is almost a way of life these days. From the frustration of waiting in line to waiting to grow up, people try to hurry life up.

That big hurry spreads to the way people are treated, too. You may know someone that, for whatever reason, really rings your impatience bell ... someone you want to help finish sentences or help make decisions!

A heart in which God's Spirit lives is identifiable by its patience – with others and with situations. Cut others some slack and don't stress about stuff. Are you identifiable by your patience?

Dear Father,

No, I'm not exactly patient. Please help me by filling me with the patience of Your Spirit.

Amen

The fruit OF THE Spirit is LOVE, JOY, PEACE, patience ...

GALATIANS 5:22

Kind Speech

The fruit OF THE Spirit is LOVE, JOY, PEACE, PATIENCE, kindness

GALATIANS 5:22

*W*hat's the sharpest, most dangerous item you can think of? Nope, the right answer is the tongue.

Yeah, it's quite unreal how much the words you speak can hurt another person. Well, you've probably been on the receiving end of mean comments. You know how the bad feelings just lay on your heart making you feel bad like no one in the world could like you.

Remember, your unkind words do that to others, too. A life filled with the power of God's Spirit is identifiable by kindness – that's especially noticeable by the words that are spoken. Ask God to help you think about the words you speak ... and not just the words but also the tone of your voice. Be identified by kindness!

Dear God,

I know how lousy I feel when someone says something mean to me. Don't let me do that to anyone else. Help me be kind. *Amen*

Sooooo Good!

What kinds of things are good? Chocolate? Ice cream? Music? Movies? Books? Think about how many times you use the word good. Now, how often do you use this word to describe another person? What makes a person good?

A good person is probably someone who is honest, nice, kind – a lot of good characteristics rolled into one. Just about everyone is good some of the time – but it's so hard. People can be so annoying sometimes.

Or, when a teacher has been picking on you, maybe you just want to lash out at someone. Being fair, honest and kind is sometimes far, far away from where your heart is. But when God's Holy Spirit lives inside you, goodness shows to those around you.

Dear Lord,

I want people to see goodness when they look at me – Your goodness. *Amen*

The fruit **OF THE** Spirit is LOVE, JOY, PEACE, PATIENCE, KINDNESS, goodness

GALATIANS 5:22

A Dog's Love

The fruit OF THE Spirit is LOVE, JOY, PEACE, PATIENCE, KINDNESS, GOODNESS, faithfulness...

GALATIANS 5:22

A little boy once prayed, "God, help me to be the kind of person my dog thinks I am." Dogs are so loyal. They forgive you for leaving them behind when you go out. They're always happy to see you. They want to spend all their time with you. Loyalty is a lot like faithfulness.

A girl who has God's Holy Spirit living in her is identifiable by her faithfulness to God ... all the time. It's easy to be faithful to God when you're with other Christians. Then you can say, "Yeah, I love God and I want to obey Him."

But how faithful are you when you're with friends who don't care about God? Are you identifiable by your faithfulness to God?

Dear God,

It is hard to talk about You and do stuff like pray before lunch when I'm with friends who don't know You. Help me to be more faithful.

Amen

Gentle Me

Some things in life require gentleness. Things like holding a newborn baby, moving your mom's favorite lamp, eggs, other people's feelings ... Wait a minute, what was that last one? Yeah, it's true.

A girl who has God's Spirit living in her will be identifiable by her gentleness. That means being careful of others' feelings, expressing your ideas and opinions in a kind and gentle way. It can be so easy to jump on the bandwagon of being loud, sarcastic and pushy when your friends are riding that wagon.

Remember, you have God's Spirit living in you and gentleness is His style.

Dear Father,

Gentleness doesn't come naturally to me. Please help me to be gentle with others so they can see Your love in me.
Amen

The fruit OF THE Spirit is LOVE, JOY, PEACE, PATIENCE, KINDNESS, GOODNESS, FAITHFULNESS, Gentleness

GALATIANS 5:22-23

Keeping Control

The fruit
OF THE
Spirit is
LOVE, JOY, PEACE,
PATIENCE, KINDNESS,
GOODNESS,
FAITHFULNESS,
GENTLENESS AND
self-control.

GALATIANS 5:22 - 23

Self-control is important in many different areas of our lives. Take your temper, for example. When you get angry at your little brother and you want to pound him, you have to use self-control to keep your temper from taking over.

How about when your mom bakes a big batch of chocolate chip cookies? You could eat a plateful, but self-control means you eat only one. Or, when some of your friends are ripping up another girl for her clothes, hair, looks or whatever? You could join in the mean conversation, but self-control stops you. Self-control means that sometimes you don't do or say what you're thinking. A child of God is identifiable by her self-control.

Dear God,

Okay ... I can't do this one alone. Give me Your strength so I can have self-control. *Amen*

Keep the Peace

*O*beying is something you will never outgrow. Well, that sounds depressing, doesn't it? Well, keep your crown on, and listen to this: No matter how grown up you get, there will still be policemen, judges, doctors and others who need to be obeyed.

A characteristic of a child of God is obedience – without complaining or fighting. God placed leaders, rulers and teachers in their positions, and they must be respected. It wouldn't look good for a town, nation or country to be torn apart by Christians who resist obeying the leaders of the land.

Even if the rulers don't honor God – it's His job to deal with them. It's your job to be subject to them.

Dear God,

It isn't always easy to obey. But I want Your Spirit to shine through me, so please help me to obey.

Amen

REMIND the people to be SUBJECT to RULERS and authorities.

TITUS 3:1

Choose God This Day

Set your minds ON THINGS above, not on EARTHLY THINGS.

Colossians 3:2

*E*very day of your life you set your priorities. You choose how to spend your time, whether to be kind, how to talk about your parents and whether or not to do your homework.

You decide if talking on the phone with a friend is more important than prayer time. You choose whether to hang out at the mall or go to youth group at church. You decide what is important to you.

This verse encourages you to look at the big picture; to see what is important in more than just this minute. Because you will grow up, your friends will change, your tastes will change, but the one thing that won't change is God. Make Him your number one priority now.

Dear Father,

Help me to choose You over all the other things that yell for my attention and loyalty. I want You to be my number one priority. *Amen*

Awesome Love

*E*verything inside you should be straining toward being a girl whose life and character reflect who God is.

God doesn't want some of your love and obedience. He isn't interested in your worship on Sunday morning if you ignore Him the rest of the week.

Read this entire verse – God wants your love and service to come from *all* your heart and *all* your soul. This isn't because He's on a power trip ... it's because that's how much He loves you ... *completely.*

Dear God,

I never thought of it that way before – You want all my love because You give me all of Your love. That's awesome. Thank You! *Amen*

WHAT DOES THE **LORD YOUR GOD** REQUIRE OF YOU, BUT TO FEAR THE LORD YOUR GOD, TO **walk** IN ALL **HIS WAYS, TO love Him,** TO **SERVE** THE LORD YOUR GOD WITH **ALL YOUR HEART** AND WITH ALL YOUR **SOUL** & TO KEEP THE **COMMANDMENTS OF THE LORD.**

DEUTERONOMY 10:12-13

A Full Life

Matthew 6:33

SEEK FIRST THE *kingdom* OF GOD AND HIS RIGHTEOUSNESS & ALL THESE THINGS WILL BE ADDED TO YOU.

You can't outgive God. That's the cool thing about living your life for Him. You don't have to feel like you're giving something up to serve God. The only thing you'll be looking at in your rearview mirror is selfishness, unkindness, loneliness ... sin.

See, some people will tell you that being a Christian takes the fun stuff out of your life. But Jesus said that obeying Him, learning about Him, and serving Him will actually add success, happiness and joy to your life. Sounds like a good deal, doesn't it?

Dear God,

Help me understand this 'cause some of my friends tell me that serving You takes all the fun out of life. I want to be able to explain how it's totally the opposite. *Amen*

Praise Always

*D*o you get it? God loves you so very much. He shows His love every day by taking care of you, providing for your needs, listening to your prayers.

He sent Jesus, His only Son, to die for your sins, raised Him back to life, and now He's in heaven getting a place ready for you to spend eternity.

Wow! This deserves your total praise, doesn't it? Sing your praises, shout them, whisper them ... just do it. It gives Him joy to hear your praises and it gives you joy to give them. It's the right thing to do!

Dear Lord,

Sometimes praise just spills out of me and I want to be comfortable with that happening more and more. I'm so thankful for all You do for me!

Amen

Prayer Time

"CALL TO ME AND I WILL ANSWER YOU, AND WILL TELL YOU GREAT & HIDDEN THINGS THAT YOU HAVE NOT KNOWN."

JEREMIAH 33:3

Prayer should be a top priority in your life. It isn't easy, though, to be consistent in your prayer life, is it? You might concentrate on giving a lot of time to prayer for a while, then life gets busy and your prayer time gets pushed aside or compressed to less and less time. What was top priority at first slowly gets pushed down to the bottom priority.

What's amazing is that God offers you so much – if you will just call to Him. Many of His children don't take advantage of that.

He promises to help you understand things you could never dream or imagine if you will just come to Him.

Dear God,

I know I'm missing a lot by not talking to You more. Help me make prayer the top priority in my life.

Amen

God Is Love

Jesus spoke these words. Don't read them lightly – think about them. God, the Father loved His only Son, Jesus, totally and completely. Jesus loves you with that same kind of love. His love doesn't hold back anything, He would do anything for you, in fact He did ... He died for you.

When you understand that someone loves you that much, it can change your life. His love for you flows from His Father and fills you. He desires your love in return and your obedience to Him. He also desires that His love for you would cause you to love those around you, too.

God's love is given to you freely, but is expected to be shared with others.

Dear God,

Everything about You is love. Please let everything about me be love, too. *Amen*

"As the Father has LOVED ME, SO HAVE I loved YOU."

John 15:9

Hurry to Obedience

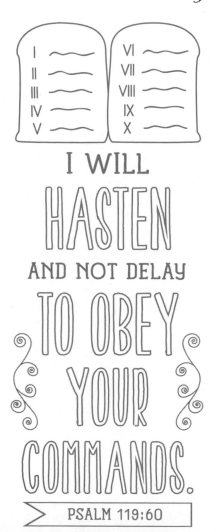

I WILL HASTEN AND NOT DELAY TO OBEY YOUR COMMANDS.

> PSALM 119:60

In a minute!" Is that a pretty standard response for just about anything your mom or dad asks you to do? It kind of puts you in control when they ask you to clean your room or load the dishwasher or do your homework, doesn't it? You get to operate on your time frame.

Do you do the same thing with God? "I'll obey You, God, and change the way I live ... in a minute." Yeah, after all, you don't want to miss anything fun by being too spiritual, right? Well, it shouldn't work that way. God doesn't give His amazing love and care to you "in a minute."

Make a choice today to hurry to obey His commands. Make obedience a top priority.

Dear Father,

I know I'm guilty of putting off things. Please help me to hurry to obedience. Amen

Unity and Peace

Getting along with one another is important. It's important enough that God mentions it in the Bible several times. His children should be different from the rest of the world because of their love for one another.

Little differences that can so easily blow up into big arguments and should be handled right away. All of the "she said this and she did that" stuff that becomes fuel for fire when you whisper about it with other friends ... must stop. Unity and peace are more important.

If you have a problem with someone, go to her alone and talk it out. You'll be glad you did.

Dear Father,

It's so easy to just complain to another friend when someone makes me mad. Help me remember to go right to the problem and deal with it so unity and peace aren't ruined.   *Amen*

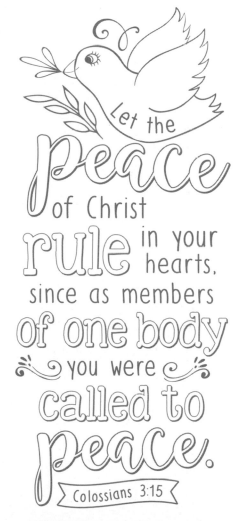

Let the **peace** of Christ **rule** in your hearts, since as members of one body you were called to **peace.**

Colossians 3:15

God's Gift

John 3:18

"WHOEVER believes IN HIM is NOT condemned, but WHOEVER DOES not believe stands condemned already because THEY HAVE not believed in the name of GOD'S one and only SON."

God loves you and wants you to be with Him in heaven forever! That couldn't happen without His gift of Jesus. Way back in the beginning Adam and Eve set sin in motion by choosing to disobey God and that has given people a choice of obeying God or sinning ever since.

God won't allow sinful beings to come into His heaven so He offered a way for us to be cleaned. Jesus took our sins on Himself – died for them – so we don't have to.

So, by choosing to accept Jesus into your heart, repenting or turning away from your sins, and desiring to obey God, you are no longer condemned to stay outside of heaven. Choose Him.

Dear God,

I choose Jesus. Thank You for Your gift of love.

Amen

Love Your Enemies

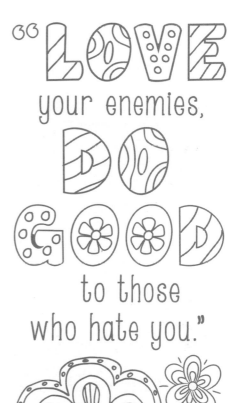

"LOVE your enemies, DO GOOD to those who hate you."

Luke 6:27

*D*oes this verse make you want to shout: "Hey ... you wouldn't say that if you knew my enemies! All they want to do is make my life miserable!" So what? Jesus spent time on this earth teaching people how to live together in unity and peace. He taught that His children should be different from the rest of the world.

If you just love your friends, that's no different from the rest of the world. If you can be kind and loving to those who aren't kind to you ... that shows God's love.

Suck it up ... don't always just look out for yourself, but show God's love to those who aren't loving to you.

Dear God,

You know how hard this is for me. You're gonna have to help me with this ... I want Your help, please.
Amen

Be Strong

JESUS ANSWERED, "IT IS WRITTEN: Man SHALL NOT live ON bread ALONE."

LUKE 4:4

Do you have any idea who Jesus was talking to when He spoke these words? Yeah, Satan! He was tempting Jesus to turn away from God.

Jesus had not eaten for forty days and Satan was challenging Him to turn stones into bread so He could eat. Jesus had to really be hungry, but He didn't cave in. It's so hard to be strong – to do the right thing – when you're tired, hungry, angry, discouraged or depressed. The truth is that you're probably feeling that way a lot of the time, too. But, that's when you need to be strong in your walk with God.

Remember that obeying Him is more important than whatever temptation is shouting for your attention.

Dear God,

Thank You for the reminder that Jesus knows what temptation feels like. Help me to be strong and never turn away from You. Amen

Constant Praise

This is the last devotion on setting priorities. Make this a major one! Praise God! Your praise brings Him joy! The psalmist writes that all creation praises God. The mountains, oceans ... everything shouts how big, wonderful and creative God is.

One time Jesus even said that if people didn't praise God, the very stones on the road would shout out praise to Him. God gave you breath. He gave you life. He loves you.

Praise Him every day – not just on Sundays or youth group days – not just when you're with your church friends. Praise Him so that all your world will know who He is!

Dear Lord,

I do praise You for Your love for me. I praise You for the world You've given me. I praise You for the gift of Jesus. I praise You for everything! *Amen*

LET EVERYTHING that has breath PRAISE THE LORD. Praise the LORD.

Psalm 150:6

It's Not Good to Be Alone

THE LORD **God said,** "IT IS NOT GOOD FOR THE MAN TO BE ALONE. I WILL MAKE A **helper** SUITABLE **for him."**

GENESIS 2:18

You may be wondering what on earth the creation of Eve to be Adam's helper has to do with you or your family. Simple – it's God's first sentence there ... it isn't good for man to be alone.

God made you. He made all humans and He knows that we need one another. You need to know that you belong somewhere ... in your family. You need to know for absolute sure that someone loves you, no matter what happens.

As irritating and annoying as parents and siblings can sometimes be ... they are your family and they are a gift from God. Start this month with that thought in mind.

Dear God,

Sometimes I'm miserable with my family, but deep down I love them a lot and I know they love me.

Amen

Strength in Numbers

There's no doubt about it – life is better when it's shared with others. Sometimes life is hard – school stinks, friends are being creeps, you're lonely or discouraged. Hey, that's true for everyone sometimes. If you're trying to gut your way through life alone, you're not going to make it.

But if you share your problems with your family you'll find that they will encourage you and pray for you. The strength you gain by letting your parents stand strong with you will help you in life.

The third strand mentioned in this super-strong cord? Well, that's God. Make Him part of everything!

Dear God,

For some reason it's hard to share stuff with my family. I know they love me, but ... I don't know. Help me to be open with them and stay close to them. *Amen*

Though **ONE** may be **overpowered**, **TWO** can defend themselves. **A cord of THREE** strands is not quickly broken.

Ecclesiastes 4:12

Cut 'em Some Slack

We all stumble in **many ways.** Anyone who is never at fault in what they **say is perfect,** able to keep their **whole body** in check. > James 3:2

*D*o your parents sometimes embarrass you? Do you think they are old-fashioned and that their rules are stuffy and unfair? What about your brothers and sisters? Do they just annoy you to pieces by the things they do and how selfish they are? Yeah, families can be a pain. But one thing to remember is that you are a member of your family and let's face it, you're not perfect either.

You can complain all you want about your family, but remember that you're also not perfect. Cut them some slack and be thankful when they do the same for you.

Dear God,

I know I complain a lot about my family, but I guess I'm not perfect either. Thank You that they love me anyway. I love them too.

Amen

No-Fretting Zone

*W*hen the wick of a firecracker is lit, it crackles and burns all the way to the firecracker itself and then ... *boom!* Anger is kind of like that. When you get upset with someone, and let it boil around in your heart and mind, you are feeding your anger.

It's going to crackle and burn until ... *boom!* That kind of explosion wrecks relationships. It's tough in families because you live in close contact – tempers are going to flare.

But the reminder of this verse is to deal with anger right away – don't let it roll around inside of you – that's the fretting part. Just take care of business.

Dear God,

I don't like confrontations with people, so it's hard to deal with things right away. It's easier to fret. Help me be grown up enough to deal with stuff right away. *Amen*

Refrain from ANGER & TURN FROM WRATH; do not FRET- it leads only to EVIL.

PSALM 37:8

Encouragement Helps

KNOWLEDGE PUFFS up WHILE LOVE BUILDS up.

1 Corinthians 8:1

*E*ncouragement keeps you going sometimes. Hearing nice things about your abilities or talents can keep you on your feet when you are discouraged. Your parents can do that for you. Maybe you've noticed that your parents are your biggest cheerleaders. They have been proud of your accomplishments – from the first crayon drawing they put on the refrigerator to any sports accomplishments, piano recitals, school papers – whatever your strength might be.

Your parents' love seeks to build you up. It is encouraging you to be the best person you can be. Think about how you can pass that on by building up someone you love.

Dear God,

Thank You for my parents. Their encouragement means a lot to me - even if I don't always act like it does. I'm thankful for them. *Amen*

Count to Ten

You've probably heard the old saying, "Count to ten before speaking." Doing that is supposed to give you a chance to calm down when you're ticked and might prevent fights and arguments.

Yeah, it's easy to say but not so easy to do. When someone "pushes your buttons" – especially on purpose – the immediate response is to shout back. Of course, that just causes more problems, like with parents, it will get you grounded. With brothers and sisters your angry responses can lead to all-out war. No doubt you'll need God's help to slow down your retorts when someone makes you angry. Ask God, He will help you.

Dear Father,

Help me to listen when I need to and to stop and count to ten before I shout back responses when someone makes me angry. *Amen*

Let every person be quick to hear, slow to speak, slow to anger. James 1:19

Good Housekeeping

SHE *watches* OVER THE AFFAIRS OF HER HOUSEHOLD *and* DOES NOT EAT THE *bread* OF IDLENESS.

PROVERBS 31:27

*C*lean clothes in your closet. Ice cream in the freezer. Sheets on your bed. Bread and butter always available. Dust wiped off the computer screen. Bills paid so the lights stay on. Dinner on the table. Cookies in the cookie jar. Who makes all this stuff happen? Yeah, probably your mom.

Did you think that all these things just magically appeared or happened? If you're honest about it, you'll admit that your mom works hard to take care of your family. More than likely she does it without much complaining, too. She does it because she loves you. Your mom is probably the heartbeat of your home. Take time to thank her for what she does for you ... and help her when you can.

Dear Lord,

Thank You for my mom. I know she works hard for us and ... well, help me to appreciate her more.

Amen

Step Out from the Crowd

EACH OF YOU MUST respect YOUR mother & FATHER.

LEVITICUS 19:3

Some things never change. This command was laid down by God way back in Old Testament times and it has never been changed. It may be "cool" to talk down your parents and complain about them when your friends are doing that, but know this – doing so is flat out disobeying God.

What does it mean to show respect? Some ideas would be not arguing about their rules. Honoring curfews set. Speaking respectfully to them and about them. No doubt this is not a popular way to behave as far as your peers go ... so step out from the crowd.

Choose to live the way God commands you to.

Dear Lord,

This isn't easy so I need Your help to do this. Please help me to remember that it's Your command to be respectful to my parents. Thank You.

Amen

No-Complaining Zone

Do everything without grumbling or arguing.

Philippians 2:14

No whining. No complaining. No arguing. Get real – is this possible? You know what it's like when you want to meet your friends at the mall to hang out on a Saturday afternoon, but your mom says it's your turn to clean the bathrooms. Of course, if you just did the job you could be at the mall in an hour, but instead you spend an hour complaining and never get to the mall.

God says that the best way to live in a family is to take on your responsibilities and chores without complaining or arguing about them. Just do them. That obedience builds good relationships with your parents and sets a good example for others.

Dear Lord,

No complaining? Really? Okay, I'll try, but please help me. I can't do this without Your help.

Amen

Just Walk Away

It has to stop somewhere. If your brother gives you a shove, your natural reaction may be to push him right back. If your little brother makes some sarcastic comment to you, you may want to snap right back. If your sister cheats when you're playing a game, your response may be to want to pound her. But ... don't do it. The cycle has to stop somewhere.

Because you have God's Spirit in you and His power and love available to help you do anything – let the cycle stop with you.

When you want to pay back someone ... don't. Just walk away and stop the fighting cycle.

Dear Lord,

It would be awesome if I could be the one to stop the bad cycle that I get into with my brothers and sisters. Help me be strong enough to do that.

Amen

MAKE SURE THAT nobody PAYS BACK WRONG FOR WRONG, but always strive TO DO WHAT IS good for EACH OTHER & FOR EVERYONE ELSE.

I THESSALONIANS 5:15

It's Not About You

GALATIANS 6:2

CARRY

EACH

OTHER'S

BURDENS, AND IN

THIS WAY

YOU WILL FULFILL

THE LAW OF

CHRIST.

It's better to give than to receive. Have you heard that before? It applies to the message of this verse. Your family is not here just to help you with life, though they certainly may do that. It runs both ways, you have to help them, too.

If your parents have busy work schedules and can't keep up with household chores, pitch in and help. If your sister is struggling with math and you're good at it, tutor her. Why? It feels good to help others ... and Jesus wants you to follow His example.

Remember that family life is not all about you. Pay attention to others' needs and help where you can.

Dear Lord,

Help me to notice when my family needs help. Give me the right attitude so that I want to jump in and help them. *Amen*

Thinking About Others

One sign of growing up is when you begin to understand that the world doesn't revolve around you. One characteristic of most children is self-centeredness. A child usually cares more about her own feelings than anyone else's. An immature person looks at every situation and thinks first about how it will affect her life. A child pays attention to her own needs before thinking of anyone else's. Do you see the pattern here?

As you mature in age and in your spiritual walk, you begin to think about other people's needs. That is important in a family. Pay attention to your family members, see how you can help them grow and make their lives better.

Dear God,

Help me see where I can help to make other people's lives better. Help me to think of others before I think about myself. *Amen*

Don't look out for your own interests, but take an interest in others, too.

Philippians 2:4

Father Knows Best

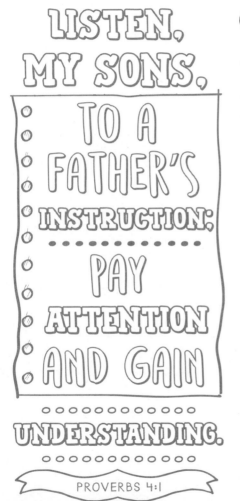

LISTEN, MY SONS, TO A FATHER'S INSTRUCTION; PAY ATTENTION AND GAIN UNDERSTANDING.

PROVERBS 4:1

Does your father wear black socks and sandals with his favorite sports team's shorts? Does he like to sing old rock and roll songs in front of your friends? Yeah, he embarrasses you in front of your friends sometimes, so you think he's about the least cool person in the world. What could you possibly learn from this guy? Well, the short answer is ... lots!

After all, your dad was a kid once so he's been through a lot of the same things you are dealing with right now. He's got the advantage of the wisdom of experience. He can help you learn how to live in this world and how to grow spiritually. So ... pay attention.

Dear God,

Sometimes I think my dad is weird. But I know I can learn a lot from him. Help me to be open to what he can teach me. *Amen*

Discipline Is Good

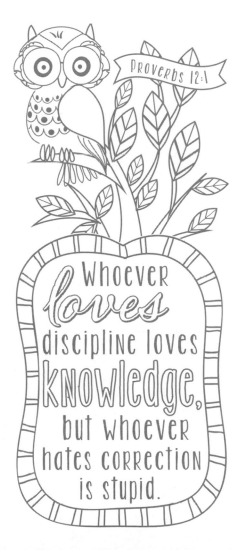

PROVERBS 12:1

Whoever *loves* discipline loves **knowledge,** but whoever hates correction is stupid.

*D*oes the word discipline bring up all kinds of ugly thoughts in your mind? No one likes to be disciplined. It usually means that favorite privileges are taken away. Extra chores may be another result of discipline.

It's not usually true that you're disciplined by being given a hot fudge sundae or money to do with as you please. Discipline is not pleasant. But your parents discipline you because they want to help you learn and grow into a mature adult who can contribute positively to society. That's where the wisdom of this verse comes from. If you accept discipline it is because you realize that it's helping you grow in knowledge.

Dear God,

Thank You for discipline ... wow, I never thought I would say that.

Amen

Learn to Be Patient

1 Corinthians 13:4

Your parents love you. Your brothers and sisters love you. And ... you love them, too. But when people live together day in and day out problems will occur once in a while. That's just the way people are.

There will be times when your family annoys you. There will also be times when you annoy them. The challenge from 1 Corinthians 13 is to stop the day-in-and-day-out-annoyances from damaging your love for each other.

Remember that because you love one another, you should be more patient with each other.

Dear Lord,

Patience doesn't always come easily to me. I guess I spend too much time thinking about myself. Fill me with Your love that will help me be patient with my family. Help them to know that I love them lots.

Amen

It Evens Out

There used to be an old comedy routine that was based on the idea that one guy's parents liked his brother more than they liked him. "He got the last piece of pizza last week." "He always gets to sit in the front seat." Those kinds of things.

This kind of person keeps an Excel file of who got what and when. There is no future in this. It will only wreck family relationships. The truth is that sometimes one person gets more stuff than someone else. Then the next time the other person gets stuff. No good will come from keeping a record of when you think you're mistreated. Just roll with it. It balances out in the end.

Dear God,

I guess if I just believe that my parents love me there isn't any reason to worry about who gets what when. I'm sorry that I keep thinking about it, please forgive me. Amen

Love KEEPS NO record OF WRONGS.
1 Corinthians 13:5

Be Fair

Love does not delight in evil but REJOICES with the Truth.

1 Corinthians 13:6

You and your brother are roughhousing – even though your parents have told you not to. Your brother shoves you then jumps out of the way just as you lunge at him. You miss him and knock a lamp to the floor. It breaks into a million pieces. When your mom comes to check out the noise, she finds your brother picking up the pieces. She thinks he broke it and starts going off on him.

Now ... you can enjoy the fact that your brother is being blamed for something that you had a part in ... or you can come clean and take your part of the punishment.

Love doesn't celebrate when someone is wrongly accused of something.

Dear God,

Sometimes I'm glad when others get in trouble, even if I know they aren't guilty. I need Your help to have love come to the top. *Amen*

Forgiveness

"FOR IF YOU forgive OTHER PEOPLE WHEN THEY SIN AGAINST YOU, YOUR HEAVENLY FATHER WILL ALSO FORGIVE YOU."
MATTHEW 6:14

A big part of living in a family is forgiveness. There will always be plenty of things to forgive. Your parents aren't perfect. Your brothers and sisters aren't perfect. You aren't perfect. There will be unfair things that happen. You will get into arguments and fights with your family members.

The important thing to remember is that forgiveness is a choice. You see, God willingly forgives you for the wrong things you do ... even if they are done on purpose.

You can pass that forgiveness on to others. Forgiveness builds bridges instead of walls. Forgive because you have been forgiven.

Dear God,

Forgiveness isn't easy. But I know I can do it if You help me. Thank You for forgiving me and help me to forgive others. *Amen*

Growing Up Right

START CHILDREN OFF ON THE WAY THEY SHOULD GO, AND EVEN WHEN THEY ARE OLD THEY WILL NOT TURN FROM IT.

PROVERBS 22:6

*Y*our parents won't let you go to parties with no adults present. They don't let you watch movies with an age restriction. They would blow a gasket if they ever suspected that you hang around with girls who sometimes smoke and drink. Your parents feel this way because they care about you.

Believe it or not, being a parent isn't easy. Someday you will understand that your parents are trying to give you every chance for a profitable, successful life. Someday, when you're older, the things your parents have taught you will make sense and you will hopefully begin to incorporate them into your own life. Then you will thank God for parents who love you enough to teach you the right way to live.

Dear God,

Thank You for my parents. Thank You for the things they teach me. *Amen*

Honesty Is the Best Policy

You come home from a sleepover at a friend's house. Your mom asks what you did. "Just the usual," you answer. "Watched movies, ate pizza, stayed up late talking." You just lied through your teeth. The truth is that your friend's parents weren't even home and you did things that you would *never* want your parents to know.

Lying is not the best answer to this situation, though. The best thing would be to not do stuff that you know is wrong. The second best thing would be to come clean. If they find out you lied, any trust they have in you will be completely destroyed and it takes a long time to come out of that mess.

Dear Father,

I know that if my parents find out I've lied they won't trust me again. Please help me be honest ... even if it means getting punished sometimes.

Amen

DO NOT LIE TO *each other.*

Colossians 3:9

Good Parents

DEUTERONOMY 6:7

IMPRESS THEM
[THESE COMMANDMENTS]
ON YOUR CHILDREN.
TALK ABOUT THEM WHEN
YOU SIT AT HOME AND
WHEN YOU WALK ALONG
THE ROAD, WHEN YOU
LIE DOWN AND WHEN
YOU GET UP.

Do your parents talk about God and the Bible and stuff like that all the time? Does it make you crazy that they insist that you get up on Sunday morning and go to church? Do you have to have family devotional time every night after dinner? Does your dad have to say grace before every meal? Well, don't complain, they are just being good parents.

They're trying to raise you the way God said they should. They want you to understand how important God's commandments are.

They're trying to show you how living for God is an every-day part of life – not just something for church.

Dear God,

Thank You for parents who love me enough to teach me the right way to live. *Amen*

Live in Peace

Matthew 5:9

"BLESSED ARE THE PEACEMAKERS, for they will BE CALLED CHILDREN OF GOD."

Here's a thought ... the happiness of your home depends on you. Okay, not totally on you, but certainly this is partly true.

You see, you have choices to make every day about how you're going to respond to your mom and dad – when they discipline you or when they assign chores to you. You have choices to make about your response to your brothers and sisters – when they attempt to pick a fight with you or are flat-out annoying.

You can choose to respond to any of these situations in anger or by complaining. Or, instead you can choose to respond with kindness and acceptance ... as a peacemaker.

What do you think would be best?

Dear Father,

Peacemaker ... that would be the best way. Please help me do that. *Amen*

Shining for Him

"LET YOUR *light* shine BEFORE OTHERS."

MATTHEW 5:16

*A*re you the first Christian in your family? That can be tough. If you're the only one going to church, the only one who cares at all about how God wants you to live, you may feel pretty lonely at times.

You could feel like your faith is always on display because your family knows the "real" you and sees you at your worst as well as at your best. Don't be too hard on yourself if you mess up — it's impossible to live perfectly.

But remember to let your light shine as much as possible, sometimes through kindness and generosity and sometimes through the strength to apologize for messing up. That way, your family will see God in you.

Dear God,

It is hard. I'm glad You understand that. Give me strength and patience so my light can shine for You.

Amen

A Happy Home

oney does not buy happiness. Some people think that if they just had more money to buy the things the whole family wants, then everyone would be happy. It doesn't quite work that way. A bigger house with a pool in the backyard, all the toys in the world, designer clothes, fancy vacations ... none of that guarantees peace and happiness. A family who has real happiness knows that it isn't the "stuff" that brings it, but love.

Loving each other, getting along, enjoying each other's company, laughing together, praying together ... those are things that make a happy home, even if you just have bread and water to eat together.

Dear Lord,

I want to be part of a happy home. Help me do my part to bring love and peace to our home.

Amen

BETTER A DRY CRUST WITH PEACE & QUIET THAN A HOUSE FULL OF FEASTING, WITH STRIFE.

PROVERBS
17:1

Saying "I Love You"

For this is the **message** you heard from *the* *beginning:* We should *love* one *another.*

1 John 3:11

*Y*ou love your family. Of course you do. But it may be hard for you to tell them that; to actually say it out loud. For some reason, at about the age you are right now, it becomes difficult for a girl to say, "I love you," to her mom, dad, brothers and sisters. That difficulty sticks around for several years, then as you approach adulthood, it becomes easier again.

You know, though, that it feels good to hear someone say to you, "I love you." Even if you know it's true, it's nice to hear. Your family members might like to hear that, too.

Dear Father,

It is nice to hear that my family loves me. Help me find ways to tell them how I feel ... even if I just write a note to tell them. I do love them and I want them to know that. *Amen*

Perfect in Harmony

God must have known that it wouldn't always be easy to get along with your family. Otherwise, He wouldn't have put verses like this in the Bible to remind you to live in harmony.

Think about that word *harmony*. If you have any musical knowledge, you know that a song doesn't consist of a single note being played over and over. A musical score is created by lots of different notes being played together – notes that blend together and create beautiful music.

You and your family members are all different, but if you work at it, you can create a beautiful family whose song is one of love for one another and praise to God.

Dear Lord,

Help me add to the harmony of my family's song. I want our family to show Your love to the whole world!

Amen

FINALLY, ALL OF YOU, LIVE IN HARMONY WITH ONE ANOTHER...

1 Peter 3:8

Show Sympathy

FINALLY, ALL OF YOU, LIVE IN HARMONY WITH ONE ANOTHER; BE SYMPATHETIC...

1 Peter 3:8

Your sister doesn't make the cheerleading squad, and she's really upset about it, what's your response? "Ha! You loser!" Yeah, that wouldn't be a good one. Your little brother's best friend moves away and he's really sad about it? Do you sympathize with him or tease him? For some reason, it's often hard to show sympathy to the people you live with.

Home should be a safe place where family members can let their feelings show and know that is okay. You honor God by being sympathetic to your family. When you're upset about something, it helps you to not feel alone if others share your pain with you, right? Remember that and be sympathetic to your family.

Dear God,

Help me to feel with my family members and to let them know that they aren't alone. Amen

Blood Is Thicker Than Water

The thing about brothers and sisters is that you can pick on each other every day ... in fact every minute of every day. But the minute someone else starts picking on them, you're right there to defend them. Siblings will always have problems getting along with each other, that's just the way it is. But underneath the arguments there is a strong tie of love for each other.

There is an old saying that blood is thicker than water. It's kind of weird, but what it's saying is that love and loyalty to your brothers and sisters cannot be equaled by any other relationship.

Love your brothers and sisters, defend them, care for them and be there for them. They are a precious gift from God.

Dear God,

Thank You for my brothers and sisters. I love them a lot.

Amen

FINALLY, ALL OF YOU, LIVE IN HARMONY WITH ONE ANOTHER; BE SYMPATHETIC, LOVE AS brothers...

1 Peter 3:8

Take Action

FINALLY, ALL OF YOU, LIVE IN HARMONY, BE SYMPATHETIC, LOVE AS BROTHERS, BE COMPASSIONATE...

1 Peter 3:8

What is the difference between having sympathy and compassion? Why did Peter command both of these qualities in the same verse? Well, you can feel sympathy for someone but not take any action to help her.

Compassion is when sympathy takes action. It's actually doing something to help. Sometimes all you can do is tell the person that you feel bad for her and that you will pray with her. Sometimes all you can do is cry with her.

The point is that compassion goes beyond sympathy. There will be times when your family members need compassion from you. Be ready to give them that ... and to receive it from them when you need it.

Dear Lord,

Please help me to do what I can to actually help my family when they are hurting. I want to be there for them.

Amen

First Place

It's no fun to be around someone who only talks about herself. You know that kind of person who always has a story about herself to top anyone else's story. She thinks she's the best at everything. She is more concerned about how things affect her life than anyone else's.

This person is not humble. Now, think about the opposite kind of person who does all she can to encourage others and lift them up. This humble girl cares about other people's needs above her own. Peter suggests that this is a good way to live in harmony with other people. Makes sense ... consider other people more important than yourself and you will create good relationships.

Dear God,

Help me see the good in my family members. Help me see ways to encourage them and make them feel important. *Amen*

FINALLY, ALL OF YOU, LIVE IN HARMONY, BE SYMPATHETIC, LOVE AS BROTHERS, BE COMPASSIONATE AND *humble.*

1 Peter 3:8

Just Do It!

I PETER 3:9

DO NOT REPAY
EVIL WITH EVIL OR
INSULT WITH INSULT.
ON THE CONTRARY,
REPAY EVIL WITH
blessing,
BECAUSE TO THIS
YOU WERE CALLED
SO THAT YOU MAY
INHERIT A
BLESSING.

*O*hhhh, the temptation. Your sister dumps your jewelry box on the floor so you retaliate by sweeping everything off her desk. Your brother smacks you on the arm so you chase him around the yard with a broom. Someone calls you a name so you call them two names ... and on and on.

That's a downward spiral with no hope. There will never be peace in your family unless you stop this cycle. One of you must refuse to repay evil and insults. Think how surprised your siblings will be if you don't react that way. You will be the instigator of peace! Just do it and see what happens.

Dear God,

I need Your help if I'm going to be the one to stop this. It's so easy to just pay back when someone does something mean to me. Please help me to respond with kindness and stop the cycle of fighting. *Amen*

November

Studying
the
Bible

Study the Playbook

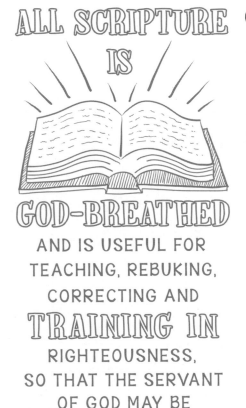

ALL SCRIPTURE IS GOD-BREATHED AND IS USEFUL FOR TEACHING, REBUKING, CORRECTING AND TRAINING IN RIGHTEOUSNESS, SO THAT THE SERVANT OF GOD MAY BE THOROUGHLY EQUIPPED FOR EVERY GOOD WORK.
2 TIMOTHY 3:16-17

When a sports team hits the field or the court to play a big game, they don't go out with no idea of what their game plan will be. Nope, they have a playbook and all the athletes will have studied it so they can do what they need to do to make the play successful and win.

God gave you a playbook for life – the Bible. Reading it will teach you how to live and show you stuff you're doing that is wrong.

Studying the Bible will train you to be the young woman God desires for you to be. Take advantage of having this playbook ... read it.

Dear God,

Thank You for the Bible. I appreciate that I can learn so much from it. *Amen*

Handwritten Message

Shakespeare was a great writer. Mark Twain was a much-loved author. Through the years many writers have filled books with their ideas about life. Make no mistake though, the Bible is not just the ideas of the handful of men who wrote it.

No, the Bible was written by God Himself. His Spirit inspired the writers – the words flowed from them as they were carried along by His Spirit.

God planned that the Bible would be His message to people for thousands of years. So, when you read the Bible, you're really reading a message from God Himself.

Dear God,

It's amazing to know that every word in the Bible is there because You wanted it to be there. Thank You for caring so much. *Amen*

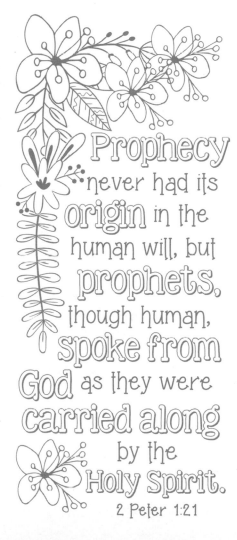

Prophecy never had its origin in the human will, but prophets, though human, spoke from God as they were carried along by the Holy Spirit.

2 Peter 1:21

Light for Living

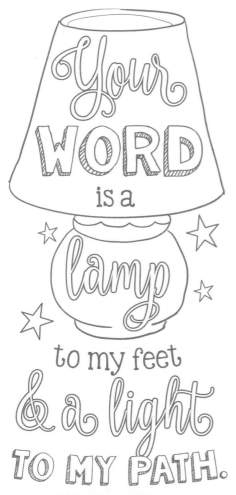

Your WORD is a lamp to my feet & a light TO MY PATH.

Psalm 119:105

$\mathcal{A}$re you afraid of the dark? Have you ever been in a room so dark that you couldn't see your own hand in front of your face? That's dark! When a light is flicked on, no matter how small, it is noticeable! It stands out in the darkness. That's what the Bible does for you. It's a light in the darkness that will show you how to live with other people and how to obey God.

However, you must spend time reading the Bible every day, looking for ways that God may want to speak to you. He will use it to touch your heart and to teach you if you want Him to.

Dear Lord,

I want to learn from the Bible. Help me to listen with my heart as I read it and to learn from You.

Amen

Day and Night

These were God's words to Joshua when he became the leader of the Israelites. These words still apply today. God knows how confusing life can get sometimes. He knows that you'll be tempted to do things that are disobedient to Him.

God knows that as you grow up you will want more and more information about how to live in this world and how to grow closer to God.

All the information you need is in the Bible. That's why He says to meditate on it (think about it) day and night. That's how it becomes a part of your life. Think about it every day.

Dear God,

I understand that I need to read Your Word every day. Help me to think about it, too, so that I can see how it fits in with my life. *Amen*

JOSHUA 1:8

"KEEP THIS BOOK OF THE LAW ALWAYS ON YOUR LIPS; MEDITATE ON IT DAY AND NIGHT, SO THAT YOU MAY BE CAREFUL TO DO EVERYTHING WRITTEN IN IT."

Put it into Action

> "THE SEED IS THE WORD OF GOD... THE SEED ON GOOD SOIL STANDS FOR THOSE WITH A NOBLE AND GOOD HEART, WHO HEAR THE WORD, RETAIN IT, AND BY PERSEVERING PRODUCE A CROP."
>
> LUKE 8:11, 15

You go to church and hear the Word of God taught. Perhaps you've been memorizing Scripture in a club program since you were just a little girl.

Hearing the Word and learning the Word is not the problem, but maybe you have a retention problem. That means when you're hanging out with your friends and they start ripping up someone — essentially wrecking someone's reputation — no verses about kindness or love pop into your mind. You see, if the Word is going to make a difference in your life, your mind needs to pull up verses from your memory bank so you can put the Word into action.

Dear God,

I know Scripture verses, I just don't always think about them. Help me to remember and put them into action!

Amen

Useful Words

Each of the three "it is written" phrases comes from the mouth of Jesus. Satan had led Jesus into the wilderness. Jesus went forty days without food. He was tired and hungry and Satan hit Him with temptation after temptation. Each time, Jesus responded to him with Scripture verses. Amazing. Jesus, who was man but also God, who came to earth to save us – He memorized Scripture. Don't you think that if Scripture was important enough for Jesus to memorize, it probably should be that important to you, too?

Jesus is our example of how to live in the world, how to know God and how to treat others. This example is one we should pay special attention to.

Dear God,

I get it. I should learn Scripture so I have answers for the temptations that come my way.

Amen

...IT IS ALSO WRITTEN...
FOR IT IS WRITTEN:
'Worship the LORD YOUR GOD, & serve HIM ONLY.'"

MATTHEW 4:4, 7, 10

God's Word in Your Heart

I have hidden *Your word in my heart* that I might not sin against You.

PSALM 119:11

*T*here are many kinds of situations in life where you need some kind of protection. For example, when it rains you need an umbrella, when you've been exposed to certain diseases, you need a vaccination, when you play racquetball, you need goggles. You get the idea.

The Word of God is a protection, too. You need to know it to keep you from sinning. However, when temptation raises its ugly head, chances are you won't run to your Bible to look for help in fighting it off. It's more helpful to have learned the Bible verses already – have them waiting in your heart to pop into your mind when you need them. That's real protection.

Dear God,

Help me learn Your Word and keep it in my heart. Then I'll have the help I need when temptation comes.

Amen

Pay Attention!

Some people say that they can't understand the Bible and that's why they don't read it. It just doesn't seem to make sense to them. Maybe they need to try a more modern version of the Scriptures, or maybe they need to spend more quiet time reading it. Or ... maybe that statement is a cop-out, just another excuse.

God says right here in Hebrews that He will help you to understand His Word. He will put His laws in your mind – that would be in a form you would understand. He also says that He will write His laws on your heart. That's pretty personal so it will probably be understandable. Pay attention, He has something to say to you!

Dear God,

I will spend more time reading Your Word. I believe You will help me understand it.

Amen

"I WILL PUT MY LAWS IN THEIR MINDS AND WRITE THEM ON THEIR HEARTS. I WILL BE THEIR GOD, AND THEY WILL BE MY PEOPLE."
HEBREWS 8:10

Freedom Is Obeying

JESUS SAID, "If you hold to My TEACHING, you are really My DISCIPLES. Then you will KNOW THE truth, and the truth will set you free."

John 8:31-32

*S*et you free from what? Well, the Scriptures teach that you are in captivity ... to sin. You aren't free, even if you think you have all the freedom in the world. You are held captive by your choices to sin.

Obeying the teachings of God's Word can change that. Of course, you have to know them before you can obey them.

The more you know, the more you obey and the more freedom you have. Jesus said that obeying His teachings shows that you are His disciple. That's real freedom.

Dear God,

I want to be free. I understand that means I need to know and obey Your Word. Help me to do that.

Amen

Look in the Mirror

So you think you're pretty good, do ya? Do you read verses about sin and think, "I haven't murdered anyone. I don't cheat. I don't steal. I don't do anything bad. I'm good." Yeah, well, if you're thinking that way then you aren't paying much attention to the Word.

Of course there are big, noticeable sins like those. But, there are other sins just as big, but a lot less obvious ... such as pride, selfishness, anger, disobedience ... you get the idea.

Let the Word of God be a mirror for you to see yourself. It will show your sins so you can confess and repent. That will make you a better person in Christ.

Dear God,

I'm reluctant to see my own sins. Help me to pay attention to Your Word. Then I can confess and repent of my sins.

Amen

ANYONE WHO LISTENS **TO THE WORD** BUT DOES NOT **DO WHAT IT SAYS** IS LIKE SOMEONE WHO *looks* AT HIS **FACE** IN A **MIRROR** AND, AFTER LOOKING AT **HIMSELF,** GOES AWAY AND IMMEDIATELY FORGETS WHAT HE *looks like.*

JAMES 1:23-24

The Revelation

THE UNFOLDING OF YOUR **WORDS** **GIVES LIGHT:** IT GIVES UNDERSTANDING TO THE SIMPLE.

PSALM 119:130

*T*hank goodness the school system doesn't start your math career with calculus. You begin with basic 1 + 1 and progress from there. Educators know that you couldn't handle calculus in first grade because you need a basic understanding of math first. God is just as wise. He knows that learning His Word and obeying Him comes in steps.

So, understanding His Word takes time. You might understand a verse this week that made no sense at all a month ago. Think of it as fabric that is folded so you can see only part of the pattern. As one section at a time unfolds, more and more of the pattern is revealed. God moves you along in steps as you understand His Word.

Dear God,

Thanks for not expecting me to understand Your Word all at once. I'm learning more all the time.

Amen

Baby Christians

What are babies good at? Crying and eating ... eating and crying ... with many dirty diapers thrown in. Babies need to eat. They don't know why, except that they are hungry. The food (milk) helps them grow, but they don't know that. They will cry when they feel hungry because that's all they know how to do. It's God's way of helping babies grow into children who grow into adults. Spiritual growth isn't all that different.

When you are a brand-new Christian, you crave the basics of God's Word. Your spirit knows that you need basic information so you can grow. Spending time reading God's Word is what will help you grow and mature in your faith.

Dear Lord,

Give me a desire to read Your Word. Help me understand what I read so I can grow stronger.

Amen

LIKE NEWBORN *babies* CRAVE *pure* SPIRITUAL MILK, SO THAT BY IT YOU MAY GROW UP IN YOUR SALVATION.

I PETER 2:2

The Living Word

"The WORD OF GOD is alive and ACTIVE. Sharper than any double-edged SWORD... it judges the thoughts and attitudes OF THE HEART.

HEBREWS 4:12

The Bible began as spoken words, passed along by preachers and prophets. Then it was lived out in Jesus' life so people could see how it actually worked. Finally, it was written down so it could be passed from generation to generation. The Bible is not just a bunch of words that were written down thousands of years ago. It is alive and active and still relevant today.

The Word of God looks deep into your heart and reveals your thoughts and attitudes. It shows you what kind of person you are ... and what kind of person you should be.

Don't dismiss this Book as being just a book. That will be your mistake.

Dear God,

I don't understand this, but I believe it. Make Your Word active and alive in me. *Amen*

It's a Battle

You've seen news reports on television of soldiers in battle. What do you notice about them? One thing is that they have equipment to keep them safe. You're in a battle, too. Satan is fighting like crazy to pull you away from God. Maybe you feel that struggle sometimes when your friends are begging you to do things you know are wrong; or when you're constantly angry, but don't know why. Satan can be sneaky about fighting, but it's a battle nonetheless.

God gave you equipment to wear in this war. His armor is based on His Word. Bible verses are the ammunition against Satan. So, put on your armor and get ready to fight!

Dear God,

I never thought about being in a battle. I want to be prepared. Help me to put my armor on.

Amen

STAND FIRM then, with the BELT OF TRUTH buckled around your waist, with the BREASTPLATE OF RIGHTEOUSNESS in place, and with your FEET FITTED WITH THE READINESS that comes from the GOSPEL OF PEACE.

EPHESIANS 6:14-15

Good Work

DO YOUR BEST TO *present* YOURSELF TO GOD AS ONE APPROVED, A WORKER WHO DOES NOT NEED TO BE ASHAMED AND WHO CORRECTLY HANDLES THE WORD OF TRUTH.

2 TIMOTHY 2:15

If you've been lucky enough to already have had a part-time job for same extra pocket money, you've probably learned that it's important to work hard for the hours you're being paid for. Your employer deserves to get what he pays for.

You're also a workman for God. He has jobs for you to do and He has given you the ability to do them. The main job is to share His Word with others.

You have to know the Word to share the Word. Don't take this job lightly. You are God's workman, so do a good job.

Dear God,

Help me understand Your Word so I can pass it on to others. I want to do good work for You.

Amen

One Single Job

God made it pretty simple for you. He gave you one job to do – fear God and keep His commandments. Does that sound like two jobs? It isn't really because the two things go hand in hand. God is serious about your obedience to His commands.

If you believe that, you will fear Him because He is serious about it. Now, here's the thing. In order to keep His commandments, you must *know* His commandments. There is no other way to know them than to study His Word. He has laid them all out in the Bible. They are there to know and understand. So, do your job – read His Word and obey His commandments.

Dear Father,

Give me a passion to read Your Word and help me to understand it so I can obey it. *Amen*

Ecclesiastes 12:13

Fear God & keep His commandments, for this is the duty of all mankind.

Living the Word

> "For I tell you that unless your righteousness surpasses that of the Pharisees and the teachers of the law, you will certainly not enter the kingdom of heaven."
>
> MATTHEW 5:20

Here's something scary. Jesus said you must be more righteous than the Pharisees and teachers of the law. Do you know who they were? They were the religious professionals of Jesus' day.

Think about it – they were the guys who studied the law and probably knew every little bit of it. So, how could you possibly be more righteous than those guys?

Simple ... they knew the law with their heads but they didn't have it in their hearts. Knowing the Word isn't enough ... you must live it.

Dear God,

Show me how to let Your Word live in me. I want to live in obedience to Your Word. *Amen*

Promised Guidance

Trust God enough to believe He cares about the day-in and day-out stuff you deal with. How will God guide you? Well, it would be easiest if He would just write His will for you in the sky ... but He doesn't do that. His guidance often comes through reading His Word.

God will make a particular thought or verse suddenly come alive for you as He seeks to guide you – it may be a verse you've read many times before – but suddenly you hear it in a new way. He promised ... you're not alone.

Dear God,

I'm glad to know I'm not alone in this world. Show me what You want me to do. *Amen*

The LORD will guide you always; He will satisfy your needs in a sun-scorched land and will strengthen your frame. You will be like a well-watered garden, like a spring whose waters never fail.

Isaiah 58:11

God's Promises

Trust in the Lord with all your heart and lean not on your own understanding; in all your ways submit to him, and he will make your paths straight.

PROVERBS 3:5-6

God's Word is filled with promises such as this one. God keeps His promises – every single one of them. God tells you over and over in His Word that He loves you and He wants good things for your life. He's not promising popularity, riches, fame, or even good grades and good hair days.

His good things revolve around obedience to Him and living for Him. You see, God knows the big picture of eternity and He knows what's truly important.

Trust Him – He's got your best interests in mind.

Dear God,

It's cool that You see the big picture, 'cause I only see the right-now. Help me to trust You. Thanks for keeping Your promises. *Amen*

No Shortcuts

When you make a new acquaintance, how do you move from the acquaintance stage to the friend stage? The friendship grows when you spend time together and get to know each other. It takes lots of conversation and sharing your ideas, dreams, hopes and even fears.

It's not so different with God. You'll grow closer to Him if you spend more time with Him. Have conversations, read His Word so you can get to know Him more and more.

Just as there isn't any shortcut to growing a friendship, there isn't any shortcut to a closer relationship with God. The better you know Him, the more you will love Him.

Dear God,

I guess it takes time to get to know You. But, I'm sure it's worth it. I want to know You more and more.

Amen

May the Lord direct your hearts into God's love & Christ's perseverance.

2 THESSALONIANS 3:5

Big Picture

All people are like grass, and all their glory is like the *flowers* of the *field*; the grass withers and the flowers fall, but the *word* of the Lord *endures forever.*

1 Peter 1:24-25

*Y*ou put so much time and energy into how your hair looks – just the right cut and highlights. You stress about whether or not you're wearing the right brand of jeans and shoes. You care so much about what other people think of you. If only you could step back and see the big picture.

These things are not what really matter. Someday beauty fades, fashions change, what certain people think of you won't matter ... the only thing that lasts forever is the Word of God. Read it, learn it, sink it deep into your heart and let it change your life.

Dear God,

I pay attention to lots of stuff that's important to a girl my age. But I want to read and study Your Word, too. I understand that it will be important for my whole life. *Amen*

Real Love

God's Word is His story. It tells about His love for mankind and His Gift that makes it possible for people to one day be able to enter His heaven. That's something that would not be possible if not for the Gift of Jesus. God, the Father, sent His only Son to be your Savior; to live, teach, heal, raise people from the dead, and eventually to be tortured and killed for your sins. That's how much God loves you.

It didn't stop there, He raised Jesus back to life and took Him back to heaven where right this very minute, He is interceding for you – asking God to overlook your sins – because He died for them. That's real love and that's the major theme of the Bible.

Dear God,

I don't understand some things in the Bible – but the part about You loving me is awesome! Thank You, I love You too.

Amen

We have seen and testify that the Father has sent His Son to be the Savior of the world.
1 John 4:14

The Whole Book

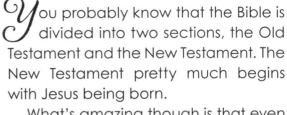

BEGINNING WITH MOSES & ALL THE PROPHETS, HE EXPLAINED TO THEM WHAT WAS SAID IN ALL THE SCRIPTURES CONCERNING HIMSELF.

LUKE 24:27

You probably know that the Bible is divided into two sections, the Old Testament and the New Testament. The New Testament pretty much begins with Jesus being born.

What's amazing though is that even though the Old Testament was written hundreds of years before Jesus was born, it predicted His birth. God was preparing the world for the arrival of the Messiah – His Son – who would save people from their sins.

As Jesus taught, He often referred to the Old Testament verses that talked about Him. The whole Bible is one big Book and Jesus is the main character all the way through – it's His story.

Dear God,

It's amazing that the Old Testament talks about Jesus, too. You really wanted us to know about Him. That's cool.

Amen

The New You

When you asked Jesus into your heart, the old you died – the one who automatically disobeyed God and chose sinful things. Now, the new you ... the Christian you, has a new life. If you want to learn about that life and begin to understand what it means to be a Christian, you need to get to know Christ. How do you get to know Him? Hmm, well the Bible is His story – beginning to end – so the best place to start would be with reading it.

You'll learn how Christ related to people. You'll learn how He related to God and what He thought about prayer. Learn about Him, and you'll learn about your purpose on earth.

Dear God,

I want to know what Your purpose for me is, that's why I want to learn more about Christ.

Amen

SET YOUR MINDS on things ABOVE, not on earthly things. FOR YOU DIED, and your life is now hidden with CHRIST IN God.

Colossians 3:2-3

Solid Advice

Your statutes are my delight; they are my counselors.

PSALM 119:24

Where do you go when you have a problem? Come on, be honest. When you've got troubles at home or with a friend or a broken heart ... where do you go?

Probably to a good friend who will let you vent your anger, cry your eyes out and complain. All of that feels good, but when you need real solid advice about how to handle a problem, is that friend the best advisor? The psalmist said that God's Word became his counselor.

You can't go wrong with a counselor like that. Spend time in God's Word, wait for Him to point out a verse that suddenly makes sense and becomes your counselor for a specific problem.

Dear God,

Wow! You would do that? I want to learn like that from Your Word!

Amen

Growing in Knowledge and Love

The Christian life is all about love – loving God and loving others. Now, granted, some people are not easy to love. But that's where God comes in. He gives you insight into a person's thoughts and personality and that helps you understand why they act the way they do. That understanding might make them a little easier to love.

Ask God to grow your love more and more so that your love for others will come more easily.

Dear Lord,

Some people are easy to love and some are not. Help me understand what might be going on in their lives so I can love them more easily.

Amen

...THAT YOUR LOVE MAY ABOUND MORE AND MORE IN KNOWLEDGE AND DEPTH OF INSIGHT, SO THAT YOU MAY BE ABLE TO DISCERN WHAT IS BEST AND MAY BE PURE AND BLAMELESS FOR THE DAY OF CHRIST.

PHILIPPIANS 1:9-10

News to Share

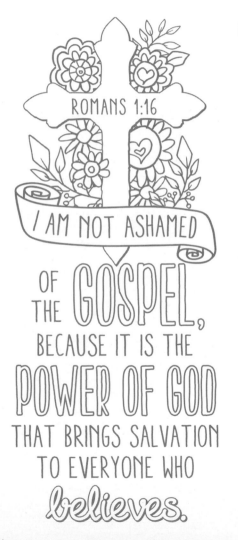

ROMANS 1:16

I AM NOT ASHAMED OF THE GOSPEL, BECAUSE IT IS THE POWER OF GOD THAT BRINGS SALVATION TO EVERYONE WHO believes.

*W*hen you have really great news, you don't keep it to yourself, do you? You probably want to tell everyone you can think of!

Do you feel that way about God's Word? Knowing God's Word and sharing it with others are two entirely different things.

You know the story of God's plan for everyone to be saved from hell. It's in His Word, which is a powerful, living thing. God's Word is not just a book, it has the power to change lives as He works through its message in people's hearts. That's great news ... don't keep it to yourself.

Dear Father,

It's kind of hard to tell my friends about the gospel. Help me find ways to share Your story with them.

Amen

Strength from the Word

MY SOUL is weary with sorrow; **STRENGTHEN ME** according to Your **WORD.**

PSALM 119:28

Depression can just flatten you, can't it? When you get really down, nothing your friends or family says makes any difference. It's hard to see any light and it's nearly impossible to find hope. That's the time, more than ever, when you need to turn to God's Word. Sit down with the Bible and pray.

Ask God to speak to you through His Word. Tell Him that you need some encouragement and hope. If you pray this sincerely, expecting God to answer, He will speak to you through His Word. His words will strengthen you and encourage you.

Dear God,

I want to learn from Your Word and be encouraged from it. So, please speak to me through Your Word. *Amen*

Love Equals Obedience

THIS IS **love** FOR **God,** TO KEEP HIS COMMANDMENTS.

1 JOHN 5:3

If someone asked you flat out if you love God would you say yes? What would that answer be based on? So, you're familiar with God because you attend church and youth group. Or maybe you even read the Bible and pray once in a while – at least when you're in a pinch and need some help.

Saying you love God is not like saying, "I love chocolate," or, "I love pizza." Loving God has obedience attached to it.

Whether or not you really love God will be apparent to Him and others by your obedience. Obeying His commands shows your love. Now, you must know the commands if you're going to obey them. You'll find them in His Book. It's a good read.

Dear God,

I try hard to obey the commands I know. Help me to learn more so I can obey more. *Amen*

Finding Strength

This message was sent to a young man named Timothy from the famous Apostle Paul. He was teaching young Timothy how to live and work for God. It sounds like choosing to live for Christ is a conscious decision. Of course, that's still true today because Satan is constantly trying to stop you from pursuing all these good things God wants for you.

Satan wants to turn you away from your Christian walk and away from the Bible — 'cause that's where you'll find the strength and encouragement to pursue these things. Don't let him do that. Stay in the Word every day. Find strength to live for Christ from the living words of His Book.

Dear God,

Help me pursue these things by reading Your Word and learning how to live for You.

Amen

PURSUE RIGHTEOUSNESS, GODLINESS, FAITH, LOVE, ENDURANCE & GENTLENESS.

1 TIMOTHY 6:11

December

Action Plan

Action Plan

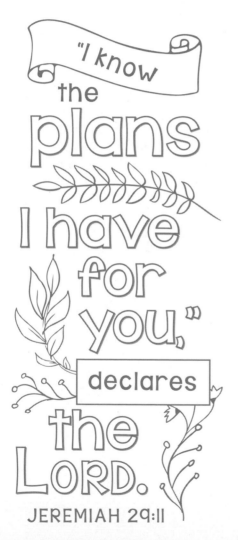

"I know the plans I have for you," declares the Lord.

JEREMIAH 29:11

Have you ever watched a small leaf floating through the air – gliding up, then down, around and around. It has no set path and no one knows where it might end up. Sometimes life can feel like that. It gets pretty confusing as you're growing up. But, never fear, you are not blowing around like a leaf. God has a plan for you.

From the moment you arrived on this earth (even before really), He's been working out that plan for your life. His plans for you are good – all His plans are good. Stay close to Him and see where He leads you.

Dear God,

I'm so glad You are in control. I know I can trust You with my life.

Amen

Be Prepared

You've probably never done this but some kids go in to take an exam without even opening the book to study for it. Unbelievable, huh? It's an awful feeling to sit with that exam paper in front of you and know that you aren't the least bit prepared.

You don't have to feel that way about life. You may look ahead sixty or seventy years and have no clue what the future may hold right now, but God has a plan for your life, so you don't have to feel unprepared.

Study His Word and talk to Him daily and He will lead you into His perfect plan.

Dear God,

Thank You for having a plan for me. I'll stay close to You so I can follow it. *Amen*

"I will instruct you & teach you in the way you should go; I will counsel you with my loving eye on you."

PSALM 32:8

A Person of Love

FOLLOW the way of love and eagerly DESIRE gifts of the spirit.

1 Corinthians 14:1

Don't get hung up in searching for God's "big will" for your life and miss doing the things He has already commanded you. God has already told you to live a life of love. Funny thing about God, He expects you to obey the truth you know before He reveals more. So, don't spend time searching for the next step, if you're not doing what He's already told you. Love is really important to God.

In the first letter of John, God is described as love ... God is love so love is God. He wants His children to be known for their love too. If you're looking for God's plan for your life – start with love.

Dear God,

I want to be known as someone who loves others, not just my family and friends, but all people. Help me to do that. *Amen*

Right Motives

COMMIT YOUR WORK TO THE LORD & YOUR plans WILL BE ESTABLISHED.

PROVERBS 16:3

*D*oes this verse promise unlimited success if you just pray, "God bless ..."? Nope, that's not what it means. Let's start at the beginning. God looks at your heart and sees what your motives are for whatever you're doing. He's not going to bless something that you hope will put someone else down or cause someone else problems. He blesses things that are done with the right attitudes and motives.

So, first examine what your motives are. If your motives are pure, commit your act to the Lord. He will bless it and you will be successful. But remember that God's measurement of success may be different from yours. Trust Him on the meaning of success.

Dear Lord,

Help me to know what my motives are for the things I do. Sometimes I'm not even sure.

Amen

Last Stop – Heaven

"Whoever BELIEVES IN THE SON HAS ETERNAL LIFE, but whoever rejects THE SON will not see life, for God's wrath remains on them."

JOHN 3:36

𝒴our future may look like a big black cloud of unknown stuff ahead of you right now. That's okay, you're young and the details haven't been filled in yet. But, your ultimate future – eternity – can be settled right here, right now.

If you've asked Jesus into your heart, you can know with absolute certainty that your future is in heaven. God has promised that because of Jesus' death on the cross for your sins, you have the opportunity to join Him in heaven forever. That's cool, huh?

So, wherever He may lead you on this earth, through whatever experiences, careers and relationships, you already know that your last stop will be heaven.

Dear God,

I'm thankful to have that settled. Thanks for telling me ahead of time that I will be in heaven with You.

Amen

A Gift for You

Play on the tennis team? No, I don't even know how to hold a racquet. Want to sing a solo in the play? No, I couldn't carry a tune in a basket. Want to illustrate a book? No, I can't even draw a straight line.

Does it sometimes feel like you can't do anything? Do you look around you at the talents and abilities of others and wonder if you've missed the "handing out talent line"? Well, you didn't. God promises that every one of His children has some kind of gift – in this verse it's called a manifestation of the Spirit.

He has given you a gift that will help His family – something that you are good at. Maybe you haven't discovered what it is yet, but you will.

Dear Lord,

I don't have a clue what my gift is. Help me to see it and develop it to be useful to You.

Amen

Now to each one the MANIFESTATION of the SPIRIT is given for the COMMON GOOD.

1 Corinthians 12:7

Your Entourage

You hem me in behind and before & You lay Your hand upon me.

Psalm 139:5

If a famous celebrity has ever passed through your town, you know that it was next to impossible to get close to him or her. Celebrities usually travel with an entourage of people – security people to protect them from their adoring fans, chauffeurs to drive them around, publicists to do their talking for them.

Well, listen to this – you have a private entourage, too. God goes before you, leading you where He wants you to go. Because of that, you never go into a situation that He doesn't already know about. He is behind you – watching your back. God's presence surrounds you. You've got more protection than a celebrity!

Dear Lord,

Thank You for watching out for me. I know that whatever the future holds, You will know about it before I do.

Amen

Plan Ahead

So, you don't know what your future holds. Begin now asking God to give you wisdom to make right choices and live in obedience to Him. Ask Him to begin to direct you toward your future by the choices you make now. Does this seem silly to be thinking about at your age?

It's not, because even the classes you take in school could begin preparing you for the future. Maybe a science class you didn't want to take will actually open your eyes to some career that fascinates you. It could be music lessons or drama classes or a new friendship with someone that opens those doors.

Just ask God for wisdom and He will guide you.

Dear Lord,

Please give me wisdom in making choices now that will affect my future. *Amen*

IF ANY OF YOU LACKS WISDOM, YOU SHOULD ASK GOD WHO GIVES GENEROUSLY TO ALL WITHOUT FINDING FAULT, AND IT WILL BE GIVEN TO YOU.

JAMES 1:5

Be Patient

GENESIS 37:5

Do you know this story? Joseph was a teenager when he had a dream that his eleven brothers would one day bow down to him. Yeah, they weren't so happy about that dream so they sold Joseph into slavery. Joseph ended up in prison in Egypt. Years later, Joseph's dream came true. He became second in command in Egypt and his brothers did bow down to him.

Sometimes, God plants a dream in your heart, but it may take a long time before it actually happens. Don't get discouraged. Understand that He's still working in your heart, getting you ready to do what He wants.

Dear Lord,

Thanks for the reminder that Joseph had to wait a long time for his dream to happen. I'll keep waiting and trusting, too. *Amen*

Follow the Leader

Every time there is a national election and a whole new team of leaders is elected, the plan shifts for how a country will be run. It's hard to get anything done that way.

It may seem at times that your life is doing the same thing. You may feel like you head in one direction for a while, then make a right angle turn and head in another direction. That's okay. If you're asking God to guide you, He's taking you where He wants you to be. His plans don't change – they were set before you even took your first breath. Trust Him, He knows exactly where you're going.

Dear Lord,

I'm glad You have a plan 'cause I sure don't. Help me stay close to You so I can follow Your directions.

Amen

THE PLANS OF THE LORD STAND FIRM FOREVER, THE PURPOSES OF HIS HEART THROUGH ALL GENERATIONS.

PSALM 33:11

Good Example

FOR WHERE
you GO
I will go...
your God
shall be
my GOD.

RUTH
1:16

Imagine this: Your dad gets a new job ... a great job. But it means your family has to move across the country, leaving your friends, your school, your church – everything familiar – behind.

How do you feel about that? Ruth did it. She was a young woman who left her family, her hometown and everything familiar behind to go with her mother-in-law. She didn't even have a husband to go with – he had died. But Ruth knew that God wanted her to go with Naomi.

Her story has become famous because of her obedience to God and her loyalty to Naomi. Her future was blessed and she found great happiness because she obeyed God.

Dear Lord,

Some things You ask me to do are going to be hard. Help me to remember Ruth and always be obedient to You.

Amen

A Bigger Job

Esther was Queen of Persia. She was a young girl who became queen because she won a beauty contest. The king saw hundreds of beautiful girls and he chose Esther to be queen. That's not a lot of preparation for queenship. On top of that, now she has a chance to save all the Jewish people in the kingdom from being killed. Whew, that's not what a beauty queen would expect to deal with.

Sometimes, God moves people into a position for a whole different reason than they expected. Esther understood that the whole reason she became queen was to save her people and she acted on that.

Dear Lord,

You might put me in different activities or friendships for whole other reasons than I think about. Use me the way You want.

Amen

WHO KNOWS BUT THAT YOU HAVE COME TO your ROYAL POSITION FOR SUCH A TIME AS THIS?

ESTHER 4:14

Nothing Held Back

> "I am the Lord's servant," Mary answered. "May your word to me be fulfilled."
>
> Luke 1:38

Mary is famous because she was the earthly mother of Jesus. Did you know that she was probably just a teenager when the angel told her that she was going to have a baby? She was engaged to Joseph, but when she became pregnant, it ruined her reputation as well as his.

When the angel told Mary what her future held, she could have exploded in anger, she could have begged for any other option, but she didn't. Mary accepted God's plan for her future. She trusted Him to do what was best for her.

Dear God,

Mary's trust in You is amazing. Her whole life was going to be changed by what the angel told her and she just said, okay. I want that kind of trust in You.

Amen

Get over Yourself

God had a job for Moses to do. He told Moses what the job was and expected him to get busy. Moses did not leap into action, but instead found excuse after excuse as to why he couldn't do the job God had for him. What Moses was missing was that God doesn't give you a job to do without giving you the equipment to finish it.

God would probably have helped Moses speak clearly, but Moses insisted on help, so God let Aaron go along to be the spokesman to Pharaoh. You can trust the fact that if God gives you something to do, He will help you get it done.

Dear God,

That's one of the scary things about the future – how will I do the things You want me to do? I guess I'll trust You to show me.

Amen

Moses SAID TO THE LORD, "PARDON YOUR SERVANT, LORD. I AM SLOW OF SPEECH AND TONGUE." The LORD SAID TO him, "I WILL HELP YOU speak AND WILL teach you WHAT TO say."

EXODUS 4:10-12

Teamwork

TWO are BETTER than ONE... FOR if they fall, ONE WILL LIFT UP his fellow.

Ecclesiastes 4:9-10

Don't try to gut your way through life alone. You need other people in your life and they need you in theirs. Often, when God calls a person to do a job or gives a vision for a job that needs to be done, He gives that vision to more than one person – so there is a team working on the same project. That's cool because sometimes you need encouragement to keep going.

More than one person on a project means there are different gifts and abilities working on it. Also, if you get discouraged and fall down, your friend can help you. Look around you and see if you have potential helpers around you.

Dear God,

Thank You for friends and co-workers who keep me encouraged and help me when I stumble.

Amen

A Chance to Obey

What job would you like God to give you? Successful singer? CEO of a big company? Famous politician? Whatever your dreams involve, do you realize that God's plan for your life may be something that doesn't seem so appealing to you?

That's what happened to Jonah, and he took off in the opposite direction. He didn't get far, though. God knew where he was and well ... Jonah ended up inside a big fish. Gave him time to think and he finally chose to obey God.

Do you trust God enough to follow Him somewhere you never thought about going?

Dear God,

I don't want to be disobedient like Jonah. Give me an open mind to understand the future plans You have for me. *Amen*

JONAH RAN AWAY FROM THE LORD AND HEADED FOR TARSHISH...WHEN MY LIFE WAS EBBING AWAY, I REMEMBERED YOU, LORD, AND MY PRAYER ROSE TO YOU, TO YOUR HOLY TEMPLE.

JONAH 1:3, 2:7

Clean Up First

Create in me a clean heart, O God, & renew a right spirit within me.
Psalm 51:10

When your mom bakes a cake, she doesn't pour the batter into a dirty cake pan to bake it. She doesn't serve you dinner on dirty plates that have been piled on the counter for three days. She cleans the dishes before she uses them again.

A prerequisite for being used by God is getting cleaned up. Before God gives you a vision of what your future may be, ask Him to clean up your heart. Ask Him to show you sins that you've been ignoring. When He does, confess that sin, and turn away from it. Let God put His Spirit in you.

Dear God,

Please clean up my heart. Show me what sins I've gotten so used to that I don't even think about them anymore. Help me get rid of them now.

Amen

Commitment

*K*nowing God well enough that you can find His will for your life takes real commitment. Yeah, *real* commitment. Sometimes you commit to do something, like work on the school paper, but it isn't a real passion of yours. So you may give it a half hour a week, maybe forty-five minutes in a good week. You don't inconvenience yourself to work on the paper; you don't go out of your way. That's not commitment.

Truly seeking God's plan for your life requires commitment. That means spending time every day reading His Word and praying – commitment to seeking His will.

Dear God,

Commitment means sacrificing my time and activities. Okay, I want to do that so that I can know what You want for me. *Amen*

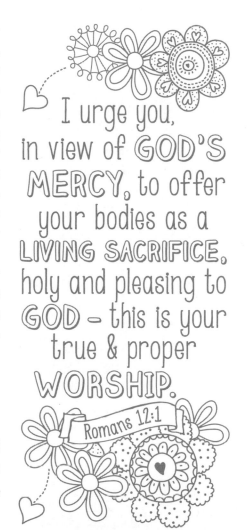

I urge you, in view of GOD'S MERCY, to offer your bodies as a LIVING SACRIFICE, holy and pleasing to GOD – this is your true & proper WORSHIP.

Romans 12:1

Finish the Race

It's a great feeling to finish a job and know that you have given it your best. You've given all your energy and brainpower. You've used your muscles.

You can step back, look over the end product and know that you have done the best job you could. Don't you want to feel that way at the end of your life? How wonderful would it feel to know that you've done everything God asked you to do and you've done it as well as you could.

What a great feeling that would be! Start working and obeying now so you can look back over your life some day and speak these same words.

Dear God,

I do want to be able to say this about my life. Show me how to begin living this way right now.

Amen

Not Just a Number

If you go to a big school you probably have an ID or student number. Every paper the school gives you has that number on it. You are not a name to them – you're a number. It's understandable, there are just too many students for them all to be known by name.

Want to hear something amazing? You're not a number to God. He knows you. He knows you well enough to have plans for your life. He knows your strengths and weaknesses, what you like to do and what you're good at. He doesn't give up on you when you mess up. God has a purpose for you and He's going to keep growing you and teaching you so it can be accomplished. Isn't that cool?

Dear God,

Thank You for having a plan for me. I know You love me and I love You, too.

Amen

THE LORD WILL VINDICATE ME; YOUR love LORD, ENDURES FOREVER— DO NOT ABANDON THE WORKS OF YOUR HANDS.

PSALM 138:8

God's School

Being **confident of this,** that He who began **a good work** in you will carry it on to completion until the day of **Christ Jesus.**

Philippians 1:6

Do you enjoy school or does it seem like you're going to be in school forever? Hopefully you understand the importance of the things you're learning and the exposure you are getting to all kinds of subjects. One of them may grab your attention and lead to your future career.

Well, at the same time you're going to school, you are also in God's school. He started a long time ago training you for the work He wants you to do. You're probably already doing some of it – loving others and obeying God for example. God wants you to keep growing and learning. He's going to keep working in you so that happens – all the way until Jesus comes back!

Dear God,

I'm glad you're working in my life. Help me continue to grow into the woman You want me to be.

Amen

Part of a Team

The members of any sports team cheer for one another. From the girls on the bench, waiting for their turn to get in the game, to the players in the game, you hear shouts of encouragement and instructions being shouted back and forth. Team members help each other play better.

The members of God's family do the same thing. This challenge in Hebrews asks you to think about how you can encourage others to be the best persons possible. You can have a part in another person's future by encouraging them to love others and obey God – and that person can do the same for you. What a team!

Dear God,

I can have a part in my friends' future? That's awesome. I'm happy to encourage them and to have them encourage me. *Amen*

Let us CONSIDER how we may spur one ANOTHER on toward LOVE & GOOD DEEDS.

Hebrews 10:24

Worth the Effort

"YOU WILL **SEEK ME** AND **FIND ME,** WHEN YOU **SEEK ME** WITH ALL YOUR **HEART."**

JEREMIAH 29:13

What kind of student are you? Do you try to get by without doing the reading for class or do you read every word assigned? Do you invest lots of time writing papers or do you throw something together the night before it's due? If you're a just-get-by kind of student, you'll still make it through school, but you won't learn everything you could have. You know, the same thing is true of your Christian walk. Do you want to know God's plan for your life? Well, you're going to have to invest some time in searching that out.

God wants you to give your whole heart to knowing Him. That's going to take some effort, but the benefits are amazing. Seek Him and you will find life itself ... and His plans for your future.

Dear God,

Whole heart, huh? I'll try ... help me, please.

Amen

Pay Attention

Paul wrote these words to young Timothy to help him grow in his faith and work for God. He had just spent a few pages telling Timothy things he needed to do to become more effective in his work. This verse at the end of chapter 4 is interesting because Paul reminds Timothy ... and you ... to pay attention to these things and to give his heart to learning them and making them part of his life.

God has given you the whole Bible to help you learn how to serve Him. Having umpteen versions of the Bible on your bookshelf won't do it though ... you've got to study it and give it time to change you.

Dear God,

I want my family and friends to see that I'm growing up in You. Thank You for Your Word that will help me do that. *Amen*

Be diligent in these matters; give yourself wholly to them, so that everyone may see your progress.

1 Timothy 4:15

Power Source

I can do all this through Him WHO GIVES me STRENGTH.

Philippians 4:13

One of the cool things about the Bible is that God put stories in it about people who said, "I can't ..." People like Moses who said he couldn't lead the Israelites out of Egypt. People like Jonah who disobeyed God the first time around. God knows that sometimes you will be scared by the things He asks you to do. He knows that you won't think you have the skill or intelligence or physical strength.

However, He wants you to know that you do – you have everything you need to do whatever He wants you to do because you have Jesus Christ. Through Christ God will give you the strength to do absolutely anything He asks of you.

Dear God,

I don't think I know how to tap into that strength, maybe just 'cause I'm scared. Help me learn how ... and thanks.

Amen

Tutor Time

Your teachers probably have open hours in the day when they will help you with assignments you don't understand. They wouldn't just leave you on your own to figure things out. They even watch your grades to see when you might need help. Did you know that from the moment you were born (even before, really) God has been watching over you.

Maybe it's kind of scary to think that He knows everything you've been doing – but He is also watching out for you. It also means that He already knows your future and He's going into it with you. He won't give you an assignment and not be available for tutoring sessions. You're never alone.

Dear God,

Sometimes I feel alone and kind of scared. Thank You for reminding me that You are always watching over me. That helps. *Amen*

THE LORD WILL WATCH OVER YOUR COMING AND GOING BOTH NOW AND FOREVERMORE.

PSALM 121:8

First Assignment

"Follow ME, AND I WILL MAKE YOU FISHERS OF men."

MATTHEW 4:19

Sometimes people sigh ... "I just don't know what God's will is for my life." Well, no one should really say that because God has already given some basic assignments. This is one of them and it has two parts. First, follow Him. That begins with obeying what you know He wants you to do, which is the basic commandments in the Scriptures – start with the Ten Commandments.

Then, Jesus promises that He will help you bring others to Him. You don't have to do that by yourself. There's your first assignment in knowing what God's plan for your life is. Do this, then He will give you more instructions.

Dear God,

I don't know about bringing others to You. Sounds like a big job, but I can obey You. I'll start there.

Amen

The Right Focus

*H*ow many hours a day do you spend watching television, talking on the phone or surfing the net? Is that time well spent? Are you focusing your energy and time on something truly important? Jesus reminded His friends to focus their time and energy on things that would have eternal value.

You could choose to spend your life goofing off, or working to gain lots of money, fame or power, but when you leave this earth, you'll leave it all behind. What are treasures in heaven, you may ask? Loving God and loving others is the greatest commandment, so it makes sense that heavenly treasures involve loving Him and loving others enough to tell them about Him.

Dear Lord,

I want to store treasures in heaven. Help me learn how to focus on loving You and loving others.

Amen

"STORE UP FOR YOURSELVES TREASURES IN HEAVEN, WHERE MOTHS AND VERMIN DO NOT DESTROY, AND WHERE THIEVES DO NOT BREAK IN AND STEAL."

MATTHEW 6:20

The Best Future!

"IF I GO **AND** **PREPARE** A PLACE FOR YOU, **I WILL COME** AGAIN AND WILL **TAKE YOU** TO MYSELF."

JOHN 14:3

*I*f you've ever loved someone who died, you know how painful that is. It's so hard to think that you will never see that person again. It feels very final. Except ... Jesus made this promise to His followers – He is getting our rooms ready in heaven.

Everyone who knows Him will be together again in heaven. So, when you have to say goodbye to a loved one, it won't be forever if you both believe in Jesus.

Jesus promised that your future will be with Him, in heaven, with all the other Christians who have ever lived!

Dear Father,

Thank You for the promise of heaven. That sounds like an awesome future! *Amen*

Get Your Ticket

You can hop on the commuter train out in the western suburbs – thirty miles from Chicago and ride the train all the way into the city ... if you have a ticket. Same thing is true of any airline.

You can settle into the seat, watch a movie, drink a soda and fly anywhere in the world ... if you have a ticket. If you hope that your future will include heaven, you'd better "get your ticket" right now.

There is only one way into heaven and that ticket is belief in Jesus Christ. He is the only way.

Dear God,

I believe that Jesus died for my sins. I believe He lives in my heart so I know I'm going to heaven. Help me tell others so they can go there, too. *Amen*

"I am the **way**, and the **truth &** the **life**. No one comes to the **father** except through **Me**."

John 14:6

What You Want the Most

How lovely is your **DWELLING PLACE, LORD ALMIGHTY!** My soul yearns, even faints, for the courts of the LORD; my heart and my flesh cry out for **The living GOD.**

PSALM 84:1-2

Have you ever wanted something so badly that it's all you can think about? Your heart aches to have it. You imagine how much better life would be if you had it. Nothing else matters except getting that one thing! My friend, the psalmist understood that kind of longing. But, he wasn't longing for a "thing." He was longing for heaven – to be with God.

Is God and heaven that real to you that you long to be with Him, to know Him, to love Him deeper and deeper. There's a plan for your future ... learn to know God more and more each day.

Dear God,

I want to know You better and love You more. I want to long to be with You every moment of my life. I want to love You.

Amen